Handbooks of
Archaeology and Antiquities

LIFE IN ANCIENT ATHENS

LIFE

IN

ANCIENT ATHENS

THE SOCIAL AND PUBLIC LIFE OF A CLASSICAL ATHENIAN FROM DAY TO DAY

BY

T. G. TUCKER

LITT.D. (CAMB.), HON. LITT.D. (DUBLIN)
PROFESSOR OF CLASSICAL PHILOLOGY IN THE UNIVERSITY OF MELBOURNE

WITH ILLUSTRATIONS

New York
THE MACMILLAN COMPANY
LONDON: MACMILLAN & CO., LTD.
1916

Norwood Press
J. S. Cushing Co. — Berwick & Smith Co.
Norwood, Mass., U.S.A.

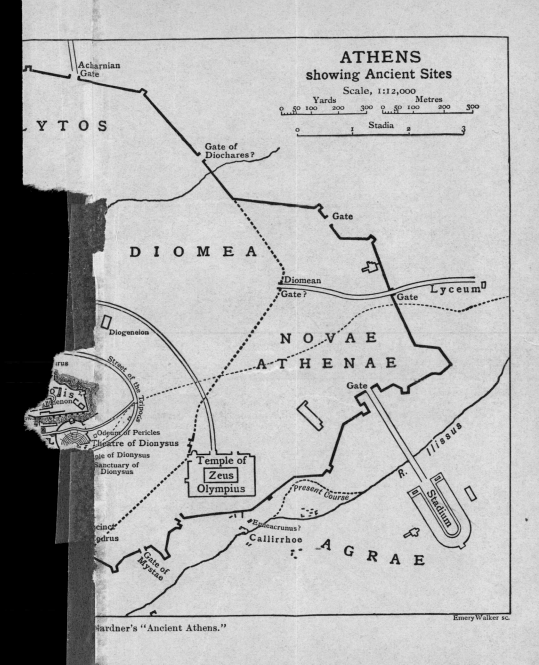

ATHENS
showing Ancient Sites
Scale, 1:12,000

Yards
0 50 100   200   300

Metres
0 50 100   200   300

Stadia
0   1   2   3

Acharnian
Gate

·YTOS

Gate of
Diochares?

Gate

DIOMEA

Diomean
Gate?

Gate

Lyceum

Diogeneion

NOVAE
ATHENAE

Gate

Street of the Tripods

Irus

glis
thenon

Odeum of Pericles
Theatre of Dionysus
ple of Dionysus
Sanctuary of
Dionysus

Temple of
Zeus
Olympius

Present Course

Ilissus

R.

Stadium

cinct
odrus

Enneacrunus?

Callirrhoe

AGRAE

Gate of
Mystae

Emery Walker sc.

ardner's "Ancient Athens."

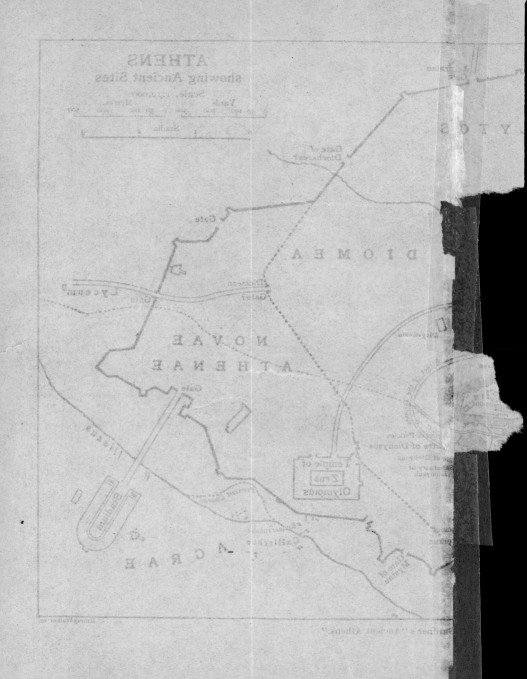

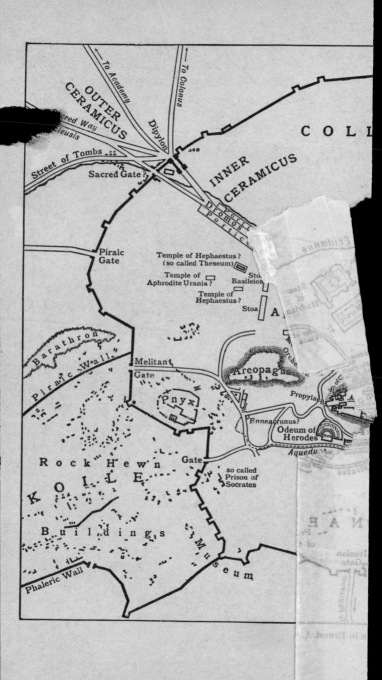

To Academy

To Colonus

OUTER CERAMICUS

Sacred Way

Street of Tombs

Sacred Gate?

Dipylon

INNER CERAMICUS

Porti Dromos Portico

COLL

Eridanus

Piraic Gate

Temple of Hephaestus?
(so called Theseum)

Temple of
Aphrodite Urania?

Stoa
Basileios

Temple of
Hephaestus?

Stoa

Stoa
of
Hadrian

A

Barathron

Piraic Wall

Melitan
Gate

Pnyx

Areopagus

Orche

Propylae

Enneacrunus?

Odeum of
Herodes

Aqueduc

Rock Hewn

KOILE

Buildings

Gate

so called
Prison of
Socrates

Museum

NAE

Gate
of

Phaleric Wall

PREFACE

The aims which have been chiefly borne in mind during the writing of this unpretentious volume are those of clearness and accuracy. I have sought to leave an impression true and sound, so far as it goes, and also vivid and distinct. The style adopted has therefore been the opposite of the pedantic, utilising any vivacities of method which are consistent with truth of fact.

It is perhaps a platitude to urge that there can be little lucidity among an accumulation of relatively unimportant, if erudite, detail. The experience of every teacher or listener will establish that point. One cannot see the wood for the trees. It has therefore seemed good to select from the available material — which is sufficiently extensive — those matters which count for most. No attempt has been made to elaborate or refine, or otherwise to emulate the dictionaries of antiquities. On the other hand, it is claimed that there are incorporated unobtrusively in the following simple chapters the results of all due study of the latest research, as well as the conclusions of many years of professional intimacy with Athenian antiquity.

Had I been aware of the existence of any book covering the same ground as the present, I should scarcely have sought publication. There are, indeed, a number of works, and some of conspicuous excellence, dealing with Greek life, or with phases of Greek life, in general. But I am aware of none which treats solely of the one most interesting and important period of the one most interesting and important community. Nor am I aware of any which has in view precisely the same class of readers for whom this is primarily intended. The admirable little work of Professor Gulick, *The Life of the*

Ancient Greeks, though necessarily containing a good deal of
the same detail, is written on different lines and with a
different scope.

Obligation has been inevitable to the following standard
works: —

> Daremberg and Saglio, *Dictionnaire des Antiquités Grecques et
>   Romaines.*
> Baumeister, *Denkmäler des klassischen Altertums.*
> Smith, *Dictionary of Greek and Roman Antiquities.*
> Becker-Göll, *Charikles.*
> P. Gardner and Jevons, *Manual of Greek Antiquities.*
> Guhl and Koner, *Life of the Greeks and Romans.*
> Gilbert, *Greek Constitutional Antiquities* (English translation).
> Haigh, *The Attic Theatre.*
> E. A. Gardner, *Ancient Athens.*
> E. A. Gardner, *Handbook of Greek Sculpture.*
> Grote, *History of Greece.*

I am also indebted for some pregnant hints to —

> Ridgeway, *Early Age of Greece.*
> J. E. Harrison, *Prolegomena to Greek Religion.*
> Mahaffy, *Social Life in Greece.*

I have felt no difficulty in accepting Professor E. A. Gardner's view of the harbours of the Peiraeus and of the Long
Walls: the third or south wall, which appears on the plan at
page 12, in my opinion never existed.

I am very greatly indebted to Professor Percy Gardner, the
General Editor of this Series. To his special and intimate
knowledge of the most recent discoveries in this field I owe
a number of valuable corrections. His familiarity with the
whole store of ancient illustrations has also enabled him to
modify and improve my own selection to such an extent that,
in this particular, the book may be said to owe more to him
than to me. How highly such a service must be estimated by
a writer so far removed from the centre needs no elaborate
statement.

                                                    T. G. T.

July, 1906.

CONTENTS

CHAPTER I

CHAPTER II

CHAPTER III

CHAPTER IV

CHAPTER V

CHAPTER VI

CHAPTER VII

CHAPTER VIII

CHAPTER IX

CHAPTER X

CHAPTER XI

CHAPTER XII

CHAPTER XIII

CHAPTER XIV

CHAPTER XV

CHAPTER XVI

CHAPTER XVII

ILLUSTRATIONS

CHAPTER I

INTRODUCTORY

LIFE IN ANCIENT ATHENS

CHAPTER I

INTRODUCTORY

OUR subject is Athenian life, and our treatment is limited to Athens. It is a serious historical error to assume, as is commonly done, that what is said of Athenian manners and customs, whether public or private, is to be said of the Greeks in general. "Greece" in the ancient sense, or "Hellas," is not the small and united Greece of the modern map. Athens was in no sense the capital of an ancient Greece. It happens to be the most attractive city, and the city of which we know most; it was the city in which art, intellect, and social culture flourished best, and therefore it has left us the completest records of itself. It was also the most populous city, and one of the most powerful; but it was the capital only of the little state of Attica, and — except in point of language — numberless other states of Greece were politically and socially as remote from Athens as Germany is from France.

To the ancient Greeks Greece, or "Hellas," meant every place occupied by Greeks, in which the Greek tongue was spoken and a certain sense of common origin and religion maintained. Indeed beyond the possession of a common tongue — although this had it dialects, often as distinct from one another as the Scotch of Burns from standard English — a general similarity of dress and religion, and a common share in

3

the great public games of Olympia or Delphi or elsewhere, it would be hard to say anything which would be equally applicable to all those whom we call the ancient Greeks. To generalise would be an even greater fallacy than for some one two thousand years hence to speak of the present "Anglo-Saxon peoples" as if they were entirely homogeneous.

The components of the ancient Greek world included Greece proper, the islands of the Aegean, Crete, the coasts of modern Turkey, the nearer shores of Asia Minor, the southern and south-western fringe of Italy, most of Sicily, Cyprus, Cyrene in Africa, and various outposts, both to the west as far as Marseilles and also round the Black Sea.

This Greece was not one country in a political sense. It was a multitude of independent states, often exceedingly small, but always exceedingly jealous of their individuality. Their bond was one of common language, religion, and racial sentiment. Of them all Attica, with its capital Athens, is the most interesting, and, to the intellectual history of mankind, most important. The other Greeks differed more or less widely from the Athenians, not only in their public organisation, but also in the principles and habits of their social life.

It must never be forgotten, for instance, that Sparta, with its Lacedaemonians, was oligarchical, stern and dour, unliterary, harsh to strangers; while Athens was intensely democratic, intensely social, intensely literary, and, for the times, liberal in its intercourse with the outer world. Thebes and the Boeotians were comparatively dull; Thessaly was comparatively aristocratic, luxurious and stagnant; while Athens was frugal in habits, intellectually alert, and always ready for some new thing.

Perhaps Athens, at the period of which we are to speak, stood to the rest of Greece somewhat as Paris stood to western Europe from the time of Louis XIV. It was widely admired, envied, imitated, and hated. In a large degree it set the taste in matters of art and literature, and to a less degree in manners; but one could not have judged all contemporary Europe by Paris, and one may not judge all contemporary Greece by Athens. We must beware therefore of turning into generalities applicable to "the Greeks" the observations which may be made concerning the Athenians. Often, no doubt, we should be right, but no less often we should be led into grievous error.

Such differences between Greek and Greek are not due merely to their respective geographical positions and to their separate developments as independent states. Those considerations must, of course, count for something; but the prime reason is anterior to these and deeper. Take the British Isles. An average Irishman differs from an average Englishman not merely because he lives in Ireland, but because of differences in his racial ancestry. It was so in ancient Greece. The Ionian Greek, including the Athenian, differed in his mental constitution from the Dorian Greek, including the Spartan, because his racial ancestry was more mixed. Both spoke Greek, both had a considerable strain of common descent, but there was between them a racial distinction at least as great as between the average Anglo-Saxon and the average semi-Celtic inhabitant of Ireland.

It seems specially important to make this point clear, and therefore, in a very few words, we may summarise the situation, as far as the most recent research has been able to discover it.

Before the dawn of Greek history, the tall, fair-haired race which is so widely predominant in Great Britain, in Germany, Scandinavia, and Western Russia made migrations and settlements in all directions outward from central Europe. It passed into Italy and made early Rome; it passed into Northern France and the British Isles. But it also passed down through the Balkan peninsula into Greece. What became of it in these various regions depended on what it met with. It of course met with some other peoples already established, and its own subsequent history would depend on the numbers and characters of those peoples, and on the degree in which it absorbed them or they absorbed it. The result in all these cases was a mixture, in which one element or the other preponderated, sometimes but slightly, sometimes overwhelmingly.

In the regions afterwards known as Greece the northern immigrants and invaders found already existing a civilisation of higher artistic and social culture than their own. There was already, and there had long been, in possession a people of another stock, shorter, darker, less physically powerful — conveniently called "Pelasgians." With these the first wave of immigrants intermingled, more completely, perhaps, than the Anglo-Saxon tribes did with the Celt in the British Islands. They imposed their language — the Greek — and in some measure their religion, upon them, but, on the other hand, they themselves picked up much of the racial characteristics of the Pelasgians, much of their talents, their defects, and no few of their beliefs. This is the first Greek stratum, and a very mixed stratum.

At least one other great wave of kindred immigrants rolled in afterwards, just as the Germanic Dane followed the Germanic Anglo-Saxon into Great Britain. These new immigrants naturally underwent less of the original admixture; they kept their race, their habits, and their limitations more as they had been. And so we have the chief reason, though not the only reason, why Greeks of one locality differed from the Greeks of another.

There can be little doubt, for example, that the Ionian Greek — including the Athenian — represents the more mixed result of the earlier invasion; while the Dorian Greek — typified in the Spartan — represents the later and more homogeneous body. It can, perhaps, be said generally of the northern immigrants that they may have been superior in physique, and in solidity of character ; but theirs is not a race famous for nimble thinking or for fine social and artistic instincts. Those belonged rather to the other, the earlier and more southern "Pelasgian" stock ; and since it was in Attica, among the Athenians, that this more native race formed the greatest ingredient, it stands explained, at least in part, why the Athenians were more specially gifted in these artistic and social directions.

Let us therefore repeat our immediate text and beware of fallacies of generalisation concerning the whole body of "the ancient Greeks."

Even in treating of Athens, our concern will be with its most characteristic or classical period. Nearly a thousand years of Athenian life are more or less known to us, with all its changes of character and circumstance ; and though events moved more slowly in the ancient world than with us, and though fashions of all kinds remained wonderfully conservative, yet the Athens visited in the days of the Roman Empire by St. Paul was a very different Athens from that of the days of Pericles, of Plato, or of Demosthenes, four or five centuries before. The Acropolis and its glories were still there; the religion was still theoretically the same; the many new and sumptuous buildings had not greatly changed the exterior character of the city; but the Athenian, as a man, had deplorably degenerated; his social system was considerably altered, and mostly for the worse.

One of the most difficult tasks of the classical scholar is to separate the Macedonian Athenian and Athens, and then the Roman Athenian and Athens, from the true and genuine classical Athenian of the free and uncontaminated days.

In arriving at the descriptions which are to be given, there is a great deal to eliminate and think away. The maps and plans of Athens generally ignore chronology, and the books of antiquities seldom distinguish periods with clearness. There is a tendency, therefore, to jumble together all that ever was at any date in Athens as if it was there all the time, whether in the way of edifices, of occupations, of social customs, or of character. That is one of the reasons why a little treatise like the present seems called for. Its aim is to present Athens, with Athenian life, as it was in the period of its greatest glory, its most vigorous vitality, and its least adulterated character. That period extends, roughly speaking, from the middle of the fifth century B.C. to the conquest by the Macedonians, or, to use round numbers for dates, the century from B.C. 440 to B.C. 330.

In the early part of this period the fortifications were already completed; the splendid Parthenon and Propylaea and other structures of the Acropolis were built; the work of the world's greatest sculptor, Pheidias, had glorified the city; Sophocles and Euripides were producing their tragic masterpieces and Aristophanes his inimitable comedies; Socrates was a familiar figure disputing in public places or in private houses; Thucydides was writing his perfect history. As the epoch advances, Plato is teaching in the grove of Academe and composing, in his incomparable style, dialogues of transcendental, if ironical, philosophy; Xenophon appears upon the scene, and the famous orators follow each other in quick succession. Towards the close of our period oratory finds its consummation in Demosthenes, and philosophy its most profound and lucid exponent in Aristotle; the grace of plastic art is consummated in Praxiteles and Lysippus. Meanwhile the great stone theatre also rose from the ground.

Politically Athens stood, during the best of this period, at the head of a confederation of Greek communities, and was enriched with their contributions. Its ships or galleys of war amounted to hundreds, and its warlike enterprise, at least in the early part of our period, was at its height. Yet Attica itself was but of the size of an English county of the second rank, being only fifty miles in extreme length and forty in extreme breadth.

In political and social organisation Athens, during this century, reached its completest form of democracy; it went as far as it ever went in the direction of socialism. Before our period it had submitted in no small measure to the direction of strong and generally aristocratic individuals; on the other hand, after our period, it fell under the Macedonian heel, subsequently under the Roman, and much of its freedom became but a shadow.

Our period is thus the epoch of its greatest and freest literature, of its purest art, of its most original thinking, of its loftiest eloquence, and of its most energetic ambition. We shall therefore try to keep its consideration clear of all later elements, and to remain, as far as possible, true to our chosen date.

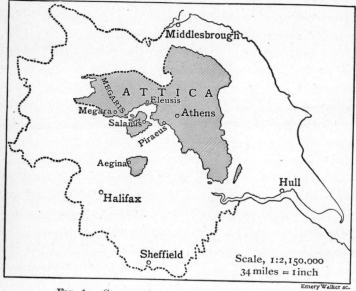

Fig. 1.—Comparative map. Attica and Yorkshire.

The sources of our knowledge are numerous, and are constantly increasing. We are by no means compelled to gather mere hints, fragmentary views and *aperçus* of Athenian life and the Athenian mind.

Written by Athenians themselves we possess histories, memoirs, dramas tragic and comic, character-sketches, dialogues, speeches in the assembly, speeches in the law-courts, books on ethics and politics. We have countless notes on public and private life written by ancients — antiquarians, commentators, and the like — who had access to a copious literature now lost to us. We have the actual witness of material remains, the number of which is being constantly increased by excavation. We have large numbers of inscriptions. In the tombs are multitudes of vases, decorated with scenes of actual life, a pictorial comment on contemporary existence.

We need not pretend that all these things, even in the completest aggregate, can make us absolutely see the people precisely as they lived and moved and had their being. There is sure to be some degree of refraction and defect of perspective in our mental picture. Nevertheless there is very much concerning which we can be fairly certain and definite, and, if we confine ourselves thereto, we shall be using our time to the best advantage. Knowledge of actual events and of actual buildings; knowledge of manners, customs, ideals, things liked and disliked; of Attic virtues, vices, weaknesses, humours, drolleries; knowledge of what the law allowed and society allowed — the classical student who studies antiquities labours under no reasonable doubt concerning the most important of these.

CHAPTER II

GENERAL FEATURES OF ATHENS AND ITS ENVIRONMENT

CHAPTER II

WE may now proceed to the external surroundings, the framework of Athenian existence.

Ancient peoples were dependent, to a very much greater extent than the moderns, upon their immediate natural surroundings. Their habits, occupations, dress, food, and dwellings were far more directly determined by the soil and climate of their country. Even the objects and moods of their religious worship were in a large measure so determined.

In our own day the Englishman may eat American fruit and Australasian mutton; he may manufacture the cotton of another hemisphere. It is easy to transport these things. The ancients, though they traded and imported to the best of their power, were far more restricted in their living by the nature of their own productions, and the same was the case with their industries.

Again, in our own day we have grown so imitative or uniform in our ways of life, that, in climates the most diverse, we build the same sort of houses, wear the same sort of clothes, eat the same sort of food, and keep the same hours, even when those houses, that food, those clothes, and those hours are far from natural to our particular environment. Among the ancients it was otherwise. The sense of national difference and independ-

15

ence was more keenly fostered. The character of a man's dress, or of his house, and the disposition of his working day, generally grew out of the special conditions of the climate in which he found himself. Perhaps that is one reason why he managed to live so long, despite the defects of his medical science.

To understand most Athenian habits it is therefore necessary to understand the Attic soil and climate. The love of the Athenians for an open-air life, public and private, and no little of their mental and artistic constitution, are to be so explained.

There are indications that in ancient times Greece in general was a more wooded country than it is to-day, and that it was consequently in many places better watered and more productive. In a certain passage of Plato a lofty and wide-spreading plane-tree and a tall and fragrant agnus castus are made to grow on the banks of the Ilissus at the place where Socrates and Phaedrus sit down; whereas nowadays the whole region is singularly bare. We must not, indeed, attach too much importance to that observation. The said trees were evidently in a semi-sanctified spot, specially tended. Nevertheless, we need not doubt that the Attic climate, so far as it has been modified in twenty-three centuries, has been rendered somewhat more arid, and not the contrary.

Already in antiquity the soil of Attica was thin and shallow. Thucydides notes the fact, and Plato grieves that the rocks now show through the surface like the bones in an emaciated body. Says Milton

> " Where on the Aegean shore a city stands
> Built nobly, pure the air, and light the soil."

That lightness of the soil, however, is no compliment. Nevertheless, by careful tillage and irrigation the country grew a considerable supply of barley and a certain, but insufficient, amount of wheat; it was rich in vines, and still more in figs and olives. Honey was another famous product of the Athenian neighbourhood. On the hills there fed sheep, goats, and swine in tolerable numbers. Oxen were bred mostly for purposes of labour, but were not numerous. The seaboard meanwhile yielded a large variety of fish.

At this point it is well to recollect that this was before the days of certain essential elements in our modern diet, namely tea, coffee, and the like, and before the days of sugar. We should recollect also that the climate of Attica, for a considerable portion of the year, is not suited to the preservation of butter without ice. It is therefore easy to understand the immense importance of wine, olives, and honey. To the Greeks, diluted wine served the purpose which beer served to our Elizabethan ancestors; it was their tea and coffee. Honey was their sugar; olive oil was their butter; it also filled their lamps and served for candles.

If now it is discovered in the sequel that the classical Athenian was a man of moderate diet, largely vegetarian, and that he combined high thinking with plain living, there will be to hand at least one weighty reason for the phenomenon. It was not primarily the outcome of his peculiar character; it was originally the outcome of his circumstances, and it was found to agree with his climate. As the stock Arab food is dates and water, so the stock Athenian food was barley-meal or porridge, bread, olive-oil, figs and other fruit, thin wine, fish, goat's milk, and cheese, while meat was a comparatively rare

c

dish. The reason is also apparent for dedicating the olive to the patron goddess Athena.

Next let us glance for a moment at the climate and its effects. Ancient and modern observers agree in their eulogies of the softness and clearness of the Athenian atmosphere. According to Euripides the Athenians " walk ever luxuriously through most translucent air." In other words, their atmosphere is the most clear and brilliant in all Greece, perhaps not surpassed in the world. The winter is brief and of little severity, despite occasional cold wind from the north; wet days are few; the heat of summer is considerably tempered by sea-breezes. Perhaps, however, few realise how far to the south the city really lies. Its climate, with an average of 64°, is that of a country distinctly warm.

If, therefore, in the sequel it is discovered that the Athenian in the streets wore no covering on his head and very often none upon his feet; that his clothing was generally very simple and light; that he preferred to pass the greater part of his existence out of doors; that his theatre and " parliament " were without a roof; that his private house rather cultivated shade than light, and generally contained no fixed fireplace except in the kitchen; if these things are observed and reflected upon, it will be easy to realise that he was — in his usual sensible fashion — adapting himself healthily to his environment.

Moreover, this splendid atmosphere has no little to do with the marvellously clear Athenian appreciation of form and colour, and with the nature of that architecture and sculpture which gleamed and radiated and blended their outlines and tints, their lights and shades, on the towering Acropolis and in every open place. Both for showing off and for preserving the beauties of art *al fresco* the Athenian climate was practically ideal.

To conclude our remarks upon this head we must add that one great product of Attica was Pentelic, Hymettian, and other marble, and that the solid base of Attica is limestone rock. The Athenian was inevitably accustomed to work in stone. Hence, when the artistic genius of the Athenian gave itself to buildings and carvings, the most admirable and enduring material was there in plenty. The Assyrian must build in brick, but the readiest substance for the Greek was his marble, and that of pre-eminent beauty.

From the bare facts that the Athenian lived in a land which supplied a frugal and simple, but sufficient and wholesome, diet, in a climate which makes for sociable outdoor life without producing languor, in an atmosphere which sets off whatsoever things are shapely and beautiful, on a soil furnished with a plentiful supply of excellent material for plastic art — from these simple facts should we start before we attempt to understand those ways which characterise what is loosely called his "civilisation."

After these remarks upon Attica and its capital city, let us proceed to the situation of that city itself. It is most logical, before we attempt a panoramic view of the day's life of a breathing Athenian, to get some notion, however imperfect in details, of his outward surroundings, the scenes amid which he moved.

What may be called "Greater Athens" consisted, as the following plan will show, of the city of Athens proper, situated between four and five miles from the sea, and a port or harbour-town, the Peiraeus, with which the city was connected by means of two long walls.

To the outside world "Athens" stood for this larger conception. On the western side, at a distance of about two miles from the city wall, ran the river Cephisus, its banks being thickly bordered with olive-trees and with grounds under irrigation. Closer in, on the east and south, ran the Ilissus, which eventually joins the other stream. Neither of these so-called rivers could boast of great size or depth; in summertime they are almost dry, and when Gray speaks of "fields that cool Ilissus laves," he is drawing upon the classical associations rather than the actual circumstances of that stream. Its shallowness is betrayed by the passage in Plato where Phaedrus remarks to Socrates " I am fortunate in not having my sandals, and, as you never have any, I think we may go along the brook and cool our feet in the water." Near to the city in the surrounding landscape are sundry conspicuous single hills and ranges, among which the purple-hued Hymettus, thyme-clad and bee-haunted, lying to the east, is perhaps the one whose name is most familiar.

Athens, in the proper or narrower sense, enclosed within its walls a space of about a mile in breadth and a third more in length. About a dozen gates led in convenient directions, and occasional towers rose along the circuit. From the south-west angle two parallel walls, nearly 200 yards apart, ran to the Peiraeus, so that in war-time communication with the port might be uninterrupted. These "Long Walls," or "Legs," as they were called, were some 12 feet in thickness and 30 feet in height. For pedestrians in peace-time the more agreeable walk was outside the more northern wall. The Peiraeus,

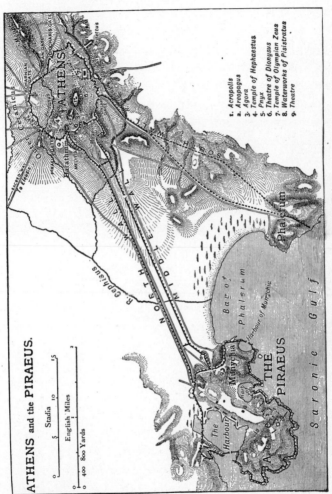

ATHENS and the PIRAEUS.

Stadia
0   5   10   15

English Miles
0   1

0   400   800 Yards

1. Acropolis
2. Areopagus
3. Agora
4. Temple of Hephaestus
5. Pnyx
6. Theatre of Dionysus
7. Temple of Olympian Zeus
8. Waterworks of Pisistratus
9. Theatre

Fig. 2.— Plan of Athens and Peiraeus.

which was also fortified by a wall 14 feet thick and 30 feet high, embraced three chief harbours, provided with quays and ship-houses and protected by moles. The most roomy of the three, which was especially called Peiraeus, still admits even the largest modern warship.

Altogether the fortified circuit of greater Athens amounted to about 20 miles, and contained, so far as can be discovered, a population of perhaps 130,000 in the city proper and 40,000 in the port. Xenophon's observation that the city contained " ten thousand " houses must obviously be taken as only an easy-going approximation. Meanwhile, in the whole territory of Attica — including not only Athens but also the country towns, villages, and homesteads — the total number of inhabitants of all classes appears to have been about 400,000. It is sufficiently startling when we fully realise that the superlative wealth of literature, art, philosophy, and social experiment associated with the name of Athens sprang from a community so diminutive in area and numbers.

In the middle of the city rose the Acropolis, a table or plateau of rock, of nearly 200 feet in height, 1000 in length, and half as much in breadth.

This had been the original settlement, secured by its position against pirates and other raiders; and even in the classical time it was still called the " City " in a narrower sense, corresponding somewhat to that in which an older portion of London is so styled. In our period it was no longer occupied by houses, but was covered with temples, altars, and statues, the whole being surrounded by a strong wall of fortification, built outside the upper portion of the rock. It has been well said that the Acropolis combined the purposes of a fortress, a sacred reserve, a treasury, and a museum of art. The Acropolis was "a dedication"; according to Demosthenes it was "all sacred"; and assuredly no such glory of art was ever contained in as little space anywhere in the world. As a stronghold it was made inaccessible except upon the western side, where a magnificent flight of steps led to the superb entrance-gate.

Below this hill on all sides, but particularly to west and north, lay the "Town," or "Lower City," of which the chief features are shown in the plan, Fig. 2.

Of the greatest importance to any Greek city is the "Agora," the "gathering" or market place, which corresponds somewhat to the old "Grande Place" of a continental town and fulfils many functions. At Athens it lay toward the north of the entrance to the Acropolis, and was surrounded by colonnades — including the famous "Painted Portico," — public offices, temples, and statues. Plane-trees had been planted for ornament and shade. A portion of the space was used for the market, and in this the traders erected their movable booths and stalls. But the Agora was also the place for many important gatherings, for parades and reviews, and for general public resort.

Adjoining the Agora on the south-west, and ascended therefrom by stone steps, was the hill named Areopagus, the "Mars' Hill," on which, four centuries later, St. Paul stood and declared that the Athenians were "too superstitious." His exclamation that "God dwelleth not in temples made with hands" was naturally prompted by the view which lay before and below him. On the Acropolis rose the Parthenon, the Erechtheum and other shrines, the temple of Victory, and the colossal statue of Athena the Champion; on a lower height stood such

Fig. 3. — View of the Acropolis from S.E.

conspicuous temples as that miscalled the Theseum. These and other buildings already existed at the date of which we are treating.

Another important elevation was the Pnyx, the old and orthodox, though by no means the only, place of assembly.

FIG. 4. — View of the *bēma* of the Pnyx.

Upon this a semicircular area of about $2\frac{1}{2}$ acres had been cleared in the rock, and here the citizens gathered, to be addressed — seated as best they could on stools of their own, or on the ground — by orators who mounted a stone platform in the middle of the diameter line.

From this hill there were visible the sea and its port on the one side, and the glories of the Athenian city on the other, and it was a trick of the orators to make the prospect play a moving part in their patriotic appeals.

Outside the walls lay suburbs, cemeteries, and gardens. Of chief note was the north-western suburb of the Cerameicus, where a road, bordered by tombs of the illustrious dead, led to the park or gardens by the Cephisus known as Academía. Here were a gymnasium, plantations, walks, and fountains, and from the fact that it was the favourite resort of Plato as a guide in philosophy, the name has passed, with some degeneration of meaning, into the English "academy." Other "Gardens" (expressly known by that name) lay to the east, by the Ilissus; in this direction also was a gymnasium, the Lyceum, a no less famous resort of philosophy and, in particular, of Aristotle.

These, of course, are but main features in the topography of Athens. Under the south-east slope of the Acropolis there was built, towards the end of our period, the vast stone theatre ; on its eastern slope lay the Odeum or " Hall of Song," built by Pericles; and dotted about the city were numerous temples, shrines, and porticoes, which it would here be disproportionate to particularíse. Moreover, statues of gods, heroes, and illustrious men were to be found in hundreds. The port-town also had its theatre, temples, and colonnades, its dock-buildings, and its Exchange.

CHAPTER III

PUBLIC BUILDINGS, STREETS, ETC.

CHAPTER III

PUBLIC BUILDINGS, STREETS, ETC.

We may now with advantage look somewhat more closely at the character of the public structures which the Athenians erected with such magnificent public spirit and such extraordinary excellence of taste, and in sight of which they passed to and fro every day.

Of the buildings and adornments of the Acropolis we need not speak in full detail. It will be enough to select some salient features.

After mounting the flight of marble steps, 70 feet broad, which led up to the western corner, we find ourselves before the special pride of Athens, the Propylaea or entrance-gate. From the front this presented a splendid façade, with much of the character of a triumphal arch, which its magnificent situation, as viewed from below, set off to the best advantage. On our passing through, it turns out to be also a triple colonnade, with halls at the side, including a picture-gallery.

The cost of the Propylaea was about £500,000 in weight of modern money. If money is better estimated at its purchasing power, the cost should perhaps be set down as nearly three times that amount. It was, however, not the cost, but the splendid effect, which aroused so much pride in the Athenian breast. Says Demosthenes, "Athens still keeps everlasting possessions, on the one side, the memory of her exploits, on the other, the beauty of the monuments dedicated in those olden days, yonder Propylaea, the Parthenon, the Colonnades, the Ship-houses." The Theban Epaminondas recognised the completest way of humbling the Athenian spirit: "You must uproot the Propylaea and plant it before your own citadel." The Athenians themselves, being a humorous people, laughed at their own foible. Says one comedian, "They are always belauding four things, their myrtle-berries, their honey, their Propylaea, and their figs."

Passing through this noble entrance, the citizen issued upon the platform of the Acropolis.

In the open, directly before him, towered the colossal bronze statue of Athena. This, which was the work of Pheidias, reached with its pedestal a height of 70 feet, and, as it stood armed with gilded helmet and shield, the sheen of the golden top of the spear was visible far away to the returning Athenian as he approached from Cape Sunium. The statue was still standing some eight centuries later, when in 395 A.D. it is said to have scared away Alaric the Goth. To the Athenian the colossal statue represented the protecting power of the patron goddess "holding her hand above us."

Rather to the right stands the Parthenon, or temple of the Virgin Goddess. The large and imposing ruins of the present day represent most, but not all, of what was left when in the seventeenth century the Venetian artillery exploded a Turkish magazine stored in this queen of ancient buildings.

Greek temples were for the most part built on the same general plan, which is best explained by the accompanying diagrams. They varied, however, in size, in the number of sides upon which columns were erected, in the number of

FIG. 5. — Restored Acropolis.

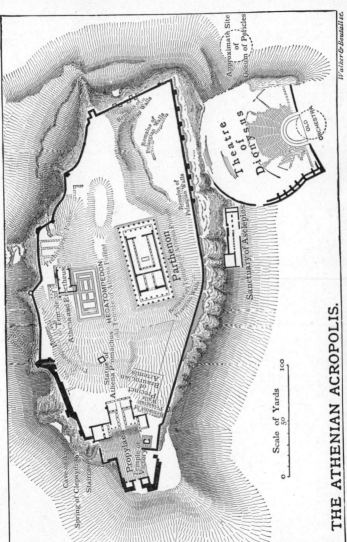

THE ATHENIAN ACROPOLIS.

FIG. 6.—Detailed plan of summit.

Walker & Boutall sc.

Scale of Yards

0   50   100

Approximate Site of Odeum of Pericles

Theatre of Dionysus

OLD ORCHESTRA

Sanctuary of Asclepios

Remains of Pelasgic Walls

Remains of Pelasgic Walls

Parthenon

HECATOMPEDON

Propylaea

Temple of Nike

Statue of Athena Promachus

Precinct of Brauronian Artemis

Temple of Athena Polias

Temple of Athena

Erechtheus

Cave

Spring of Clepsydra

Staircase

rows of such columns, and in the quantity and skill of sculptured decoration. In general a rectangular edifice of stone — the temple proper — stood upon a platform, and might have at one end, at both ends, or on all four sides, a row, or more than one row, of pillars. The rectangular building might be divided into two portions, the one being the shrine containing the statue, the other a rear-chapel, used particularly for a treasury. In the Parthenon the shrine is 100 feet in length, and it contained the colossal gold and ivory statue of Athena the Virgin, nearly 40 feet in height. It was divided into three naves and was apparently lighted by openings in the roof, and by the transparent and reflecting quality of the marble in the ceiling and around. Behind was a treasury, and around the whole were columns, 34 feet high and 6 feet in diameter, arranged as in the diagram.

The front elevation of a typical Greek temple shows a gable or pediment, of which the flat space, or tympanum, is occupied by sculpture, often more than life-size. Over each angle of the gable is erected an ornament, such as a tripod. Below the gable there are sculptures in relief along the frieze, and, in cases where a row of columns surrounds the temple, there may be further sculptures, running round an inner frieze beneath the ceiling of the colonnade. So far as they have survived, the sculptures of the Parthenon — which were partly superintended by Pheidias — are the admiration of the world, many of them, chiefly from the frieze, being familiar in the shape of the Elgin Marbles. It was only at a later time that golden shields also formed a part of the decoration of the outer entablature.

The beauty of the Parthenon and similar buildings was the beauty of great conception, and yet of sublime simplicity of mass and majesty. It depended mainly on studied proportion, which gave the greatest value to line. So carefully was true effect studied by the Greek architect, that both the platform and the pillars will be found to have a curving outline, determined on optical principles, and infinitely more grateful to the eye than a combination of lines rigidly straight. The various structures on the Acropolis, as the plan will show, were not built monotonously in line with each other. When looked at from below, perfect symmetry would have been less effective for the whole, and would have destroyed the individuality of the parts. A certain tasteful "asymmetry" obviously increases the significance of each building, besides more agreeably blending the masses of light and shade. A peculiar and elegant exception to the ordinary type of temple must be noted in the case of the composite Erechtheum.

If we now conceive of all this as bathed in the brilliance of the Attic atmosphere, whether morning glow or midday splendour or mild evening tints; if we imagine the shine of white marble, painted sculptures and gold; if we realise that all the lines and colours and proportions have been conceived and executed with an eye to this effect; if we remember that on the Acropolis alone was expended, besides the utmost genius of man, the equivalent of perhaps six or seven million pounds of our money; and if we then bethink ourselves that the men who called for it, wrought it, and paid for it, were content themselves to live in houses which we should despise, we may deduce some conception of their public spirit, their religious spirit, and their artistic spirit.

We can hardly find the space to deal much further with the public buildings of classical Athens. But since colonnades

Fig. 7.— Parthenon (present state).

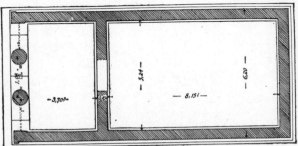

Fig. 8. — Temple: simple form.

have been frequently mentioned, we may make one or two notes upon their nature.

These structures played a conspicuous part in Greek life. What the Greeks called a *Stoa* is not a porch, but a covered colonnade, a glorified verandah. Those who know the famous *loggia* at Florence will have some, though not a strictly accurate, conception of its character. In its simplest form it consisted of a roof supported in front by a row of columns, and at the back by a wall. You thus obtain a covered walk or lounge, open to the air and warmth, but protected from rain and wind. Whichever way the sun shone or the wind blew your Athenian could always find a portico facing so that he could walk or sit in comfort. Sometimes the portico was double, that is to say, there was a wall down the middle with a colonnade on each side. Occasionally, though we are not sure of an instance at our date in Athens, it had two stories. Sometimes, instead of the wall, there were interior rows of colonnades, so as to form aisles of pillars.

In the more important cases the whole would be constructed magnificently in marble, adorned in front with statues, and, on the edge of the roof, with both statues and other ornaments. Shields or other trophies were sometimes suspended in or on the building, and the walls were often painted with historical or mythological scenes. What has been so misleadingly called the Painted " Porch "—the famous resort of the Stoics, whence they derive their name—was such a colonnade, with great battle paintings by Polygnotus and others.

The porticoes served as lounges, walks, places of resort for conversation and philosophical discussion; they were sometimes used for law courts *al fresco*, or as halls of meeting, and, especially in the port town of Peiraeus, they were used for corn exchanges and the like. In some such porticoes, presumably of less pretensions, it would appear that fires were lighted in winter, so that the poor or unoccupied of the city might not miss the accustomed consolation of society and conversation.

One other note upon buildings is perhaps necessary. It has already been remarked that the theatre, the place of Assembly, and the court of the Areopagus, were open to the sky: the colonnades had their flat roofs, like the houses. Were there no covered public buildings besides the temples? In this respect the Athenians suited every building to its purpose, and we may instance the Odeum, or Hall of Song. For the hearing of musical competitions and recitals, and for the chanted recitations of the rhapsodes, it was plainly necessary to possess a covered hall or theatre, and the Odeum or Hall of Song was, unlike almost every other building in Athens, covered with a conical dome. Pericles, who built the one chiefly in use at our date, possessed a cranium shaped like a cone, and it was a joke of comedy — or what we should now call the comic press — to speak of Pericles' cranium as his "Hall of Song."

We might be tempted to walk in imagination through the gate from the Academy and Cerameicus, along between the parallel lines of porticoes, into the Agora or great "Square," across which we should look, between other colonnades and rows of plane-trees, under a triumphal arch and between statues of gods and heroes, at the Senate House and the "Rotunda" Hall of Administration. But our scope hardly permits of pleasant excursions like these.

FIG. 9. — Temple of Zeus at Olympia: façade and interior.

Apart from the public buildings, gardens, open places, and the constant visions of architectural and sculptural splendours, the outward Athens boasted at our period, its period of greatest

FIG. 10. — Section of Parthenon showing frieze and metopes.

grandeur and finest civilisation, no magnificence of streets or private houses. There were no palaces, nor great mansions. Of the insignificance of the private dwellings we have to speak hereafter. They were mostly flat-roofed, and presented to the street a singularly poor and unattractive exterior. Their wooden framework, or framework of unburnt bricks, might be plastered or stuccoed, possibly tinted, but without any claims to beauty. A Greek writer, Dicaearchus, of the epoch we are considering, says that Athens is "dusty and not well supplied with water, badly laid out on account of its antiquity, the majority of the houses mean, and only a few good. A stranger,

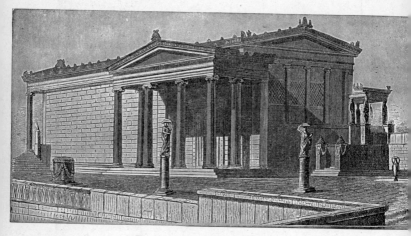

FIG. 11.— Erechtheum, restored.

at the first view, might doubt if this were Athens" — but he would only doubt till he looked at the theatre and the other superb public edifices. There we have, indeed, the truth. The town of Athens, like all old towns, grew up fitfully and without design. Hence the streets were mostly extremely narrow and crooked; many were mere lanes; no few were little better than passages. There were one or two more roomy, such as that from Cerameicus, but on the whole they closely resembled the streets and alleys in the oldest parts of the oldest towns which may still be seen in Italy.

In the harbour-town of Peiraeus, which was comparatively new and offered a clear field, the streets were laid out by direction of Themistocles on a systematic plan by a certain Hippodamus, the Hausmann of the day. They were broad,

Fig. 12. — So-called Theseum.

and intersected each other at right angles. It is to be remembered, in passing, that the use of carriages was almost unknown inside Athens itself.

Nor were these streets kept either tolerably paved or tolerably clean. That the worship of great art and intellectuality is compatible with the toleration of great discomfort and dirt is known to any observer. It is a pity; for it affords the Philistine an utterly illogical handle for abuse of art itself. So far as

E

Athens was concerned, we find none of the Roman systematic pavement or reticulation of water-supply and drainage. The ancient geographer Strabo remarks that "the Greeks attended chiefly to beauty and fortification, harbours, and a fertile soil; the Romans to pavement of streets and water-supply and sewers." There was but little paving in Athens and there were no sidewalks. In Aristophanes the short-sighted old men grope their way along complaining of the mud and clay. There was, of course, no lighting of the streets at night; as in old London, it was necessary to carry torches or horn-lanterns, except when there was a moon. It is also a pity to have to say that the public streets were anything but respected by the householders. Slops and garbage of the worst description were cheerfully thrown into the road, and just as the old Edinburgh people, emptying their dirty water from the windows, were wont to call out "Gardy-loo" (*gardez l'eau*), so the Athenians thought themselves free of blame if they cried out *existo*, "stand out of the way," on such occasions. There existed, it is true, a board of metropolitan officers, but their chief duty was to prevent encroachment and obstruction to the roads and the traffic, and though they apparently employed a number of scavengers, there can be no manner of doubt that the back streets of Athens were deplorably unsightly and unfragrant.

That the city possessed a large covered drain and a number of others is certain; but the whole question of Athenian sanitation is one of great obscurity. Let us be content to know that it was far from ideal, and that Athens once at least suffered from a plague of which it is more horrible to read in the terse narrative of Thucydides than it is to read of the plague of London in the pages of Defoe.

As Strabo remarked, the water-supply was far from being
organised like the Roman.   Nevertheless the defect has been
exaggerated.   Besides natural springs, there have been discov-

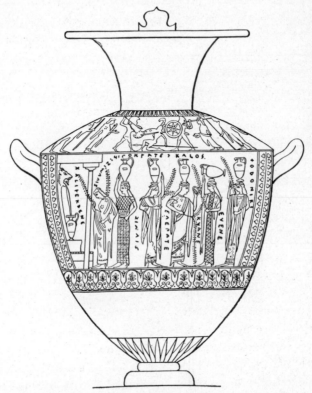

Fig. 13.— View of public fountain, Callirrhoe, from a vase.

ered underground conduits of unquestionable antiquity, and a
fair supply of water was regularly drawn from the upper Ilissus
and from Mount Hymettus by this means.   Yet neither this water
nor any other public supply was carried to individual houses.

If the inhabitants could not provide for themselves by means of wells and tanks (which were very numerous in Athens) they went, or sent their slaves, to fetch water in large earthenware jars from the public springs or fountains. True to their policy of beautifying whatever was public property, the Athenians would take a natural fountain, make a well-head of it, build thereover an edifice of artistic form, and then cause that head of water to flow through pipes and issue from the wall through lions' heads, or some other of those ornamental shapes which we have borrowed from them and for the most part conventionalised into ugliness. The chief such fountain in Athens was the famous "Nine-pipes," which thus covered and distributed what had once been the open natural spring Callirrhoe, the "fair-flowing." With a mixture of piety and shrewdness, a fountain was dedicated to some deity or hero, and thus secured by superstition, if by nothing else, against defilement. Over the water-supply there was a board of overseers, and, so far as the evidence goes, Athens was never seriously affected by any difficulty in satisfying its needs.

We must not forget to explain concerning the streets that there was no consistent method of naming them. Sometimes a street was familiarly known by some trade specially carried on in it, such as the "Cabinet-makers' Road" or the "Road of the Sculptors of Hermae," much as old London had its Fellmongers' Lane and the like. "Tripod Street" was so called from the series of tripods which had been dedicated by various victors in the dramatic contests. Others were known from some temple in them, e.g. the "Street of Hestia"—as we might say "St. John's" or "St. James' Street." A few local divisions or quarters of the town — originally separate villages — had also their names, "Collytus" or "Melite," much as we speak of Kensington or Marylebone; and it was generally found sufficient address for a particular house, if one said that it was in such and such a quarter, near to such and such a temple or public building or statue, on the left-hand side. It remained for you to find the approximate locality, and then to make inquiries in the shops (a method still not unknown) or of passers-by. Athens was a comparatively small town, a town where men lived publicly and sociably, and there was little practical difficulty in finding any house required.

CHAPTER IV

CITIZENS, OUTLANDERS, SLAVES: WOMEN

CHAPTER IV

CITIZENS, OUTLANDERS, SLAVES: WOMEN

WE have now taken a general survey of the outward environment of an Athenian citizen's life, of his town and the public buildings and streets among which he lived and moved and had his being. Assuming that we have in our minds some picture of those surroundings, let us now cast our eyes in a survey, equally general and comprehensive, over the inhabitants of Athens themselves. That population contained various strata, between which there were wide differences from both a political and social point of view. Conversation, even with well-informed persons, will show that there exist many misconceptions as to the constitution of Athenian society in this respect. We must therefore in this case, as before, begin at the beginning, and be entirely clear and simple, even at the sacrifice of some of the detail which, to the professional scholar, doubtless has its importance, but which is here unessential.

If, as strangers, we could look down upon the people moving about in their private capacity in the streets and squares of the city, or at work in the shops, the market, and the houses, we should have little outward indication that out of every eight or nine persons there would be on the average two persons of one particular class, five or six of another class, and one of yet a third class. Two persons, let us say, are

57

Athenian citizens or burgesses — "Athenians" in the strict and proper sense — counted among the franchised owners and administrators of the whole state. Five or six persons are slaves; not men of colour, nor otherwise physically remote from the Athenian, but yet servants, and servants only, men without freedom of action to go or come, men without any voice whatever in the affairs of the country. The one remaining person of the eight or nine is entirely free to go and come; he is his own master; he may be, and often is, both rich and respected; nevertheless, he possesses no voice in politics, can hold no office, and is under various other disabilities; he pays an annual poll-tax for being permitted to live amid the advantages and under the protection of Athens. The man is a "metic," that is to say a man from abroad, who has settled in Athens: he is a "resident alien," an "Outlander."

There was little, if any, outward indication of the respective status of these persons. The slave was not compelled, as at Sparta, to wear a particular dress, nor to crop his hair remarkably close. He was not a black or coloured man — although there may have been a few Ethiopians in such a capacity at Athens — for slaves came from anywhere within reasonable reach of Athenian trading. He would for the most part look like any other of the poorer inhabitants of the city. If a man of humble standing was red or yellow-haired — in which case his familiar name was apt to be "Redhead" or "Tawny" — he was often, but not necessarily, a slave from a more northern part of Europe; but, generally speaking, if you saw two men hard at work as shoemakers or copper-smiths, you would have no immediate means of distinguishing which was a free and independent Athenian burgher and which was a slave.

This is an essential point which must be forced home, a point which is of the first moment when we come to speak later of Athens as a democracy,—that the first stratum, the class of true and full Athenian citizens, was made up of men of all degrees of wealth and poverty, men rich and men very poor, men who possessed full leisure and many slaves, and men who not only possessed no slave, but who performed the same manual labour, skilled or unskilled, as might be at the same time performed by the slaves of richer men. If therefore—to revert to our imaginary case—you were able to look down into the everyday streets, you would generally be in no position to distinguish the artisan or labouring citizen from the artisan or labouring slave; nor could you necessarily tell whether yonder young woman fetching water on her head from the city fountain was a slave handmaid or the hard-working daughter of a poor Athenian house.

We must not, indeed, push this statement further than the truth. Do you see a man richly clad, or with a person scrupulously groomed? Then of course he is not a worker, and therefore not a slave, although, for all you yet know, he may once have been such. He is either one of the well-to-do citizens, or else a resident alien, a prosperous "Outlander." Do you see a man with obviously nothing to do, lounging and talking in the porticoes, greeted by well-dressed passers-by, even if he is not particularly well dressed himself? Then he is not a slave, for slaves have neither the time to lounge nor the pretensions to associate with Athenian gentlemen. Do you see a soldier? Then you see an Athenian burgher, or, if it is war-time, and he is not a cavalryman, he may be an Outlander, but he cannot be a slave.

This is all true enough. A slave, while a slave, could not be rich or idle or a soldier; nevertheless he might very well pass as a poor and busy Athenian civilian.

But let us, on the other hand, suppose ourselves to be looking on some day when the Assembly is holding a meeting. Up to the hill called the Pnyx, and into the large semicircular enclosure, there go streaming five or six thousand men, and perhaps more, from all parts of Athens and its harbour-town and the neighbouring country. Rich men and poor men, landowners and peasants, merchants and retail-dealers, men of leisure and blacksmiths, poets and shoemakers, sculptors and fishmongers, artists and sausage-sellers, men with white hands and men with black hands; up they go, with equal votes, with an equal right to speak and to be heard, and possibly with equal ability as thinkers and orators. Then certainly you may be sure of one thing, that not one of these is a slave. But you must by no means assume that all those who stay below are slaves. Many of them are citizens, too busy, or too indifferent, or even too superior, to attend. Not even the fee which they are to receive will attract them. Others again are the Outlanders, who have no business with politics. Yet of those who do go you may be sure — as you could hardly be sure elsewhere, except when politics and trials are toward— that they are the true and genuine burghers of Athens. Let this serve as our first hint of what precisely is meant by Athenian democracy. Whether the term is a fair and adequate one, is a point which should become clearer as we proceed further in this treatise. Meanwhile it should be remembered

that it was a gathering like this which commissioned Pheidias
and his staff to adorn the Parthenon, and which demanded
that city glorious and beautiful, of which a general description
has been given.

Perhaps, thus far, we have achieved one simple object.
That object has been to destroy a common but ludicrous notion, that the Athenians proper were all aristocrats, all alike
leisured, all alike cultured, and all alike maintained by the
labour of slaves. The only respect in which they were all
alike is that they possessed the rights and privileges of citizens,
while slaves and domiciled aliens did not.

After this rapid general survey, let us return to consider
each class of the population in somewhat fuller, and perhaps
more interesting, particulars.

Though we are not yet dealing with the Athenian system
of government, it is necessary that at this point we should
make tolerably clear the Athenian conception of a "state."
It is possible that in our large modern communities we have
realised no very exact notion of the relations of ourselves to
the state, or of the state to ourselves, nor is it here our
business to discuss the question. Our concern is with Athens,
be Athens never so wrong.

To the Athenian, then, the state was a sort of partnership for mutual benefit, that benefit being the safety and
comfort of the common life. The full citizen was a sort of
partner, and had an equal voice at those meetings for mutual
interest which were called meetings of the Assembly, or which
went by other names. If the state was in danger, all the
partners must defend it by military service; if it was enriched,

all the partners were entitled to some kind of advantage, direct or indirect; it was every partner's concern to make the common property splendid, and the common life safe from violence or injustice.

Such, very roughly, was the Athenian's notion of his relations to the state. And he insisted upon being a full partner. There was very little which escaped the clear view of Aristotle, and he perceived that the carrying out of these Athenian principles depended on two things—the deliberations of the Assembly and the administration of justice. A "citizen" is defined as one who has the right to vote in the decisions of the Assembly and also in the decisions of the law-courts. Wealth or other circumstances have nothing to do with his claim; that claim came to him at his birth; sometimes, but rarely, it comes by public adoption.

In the whole country of Attica there were perhaps 25,000 adult male citizens, or, with their wives and families, 100,000 burgesses in all. There were (we cannot be very exact) probably 10,000 adult Outlanders, mostly living in Athens itself and particularly in the Peiraeus or harbour-town; and the number of slaves in the whole state has been calculated at over 300,000, although there is reason to think this estimate excessive.

Inasmuch as, for public consideration, the women and children citizens or burgesses do not count, we have some 25,000 of what we may call full partners in that great association known as the Athenian state: to them, and them alone, belonged the duties and the privileges of guiding that state and reaping its benefits; and exceedingly jealous were they of their standing and their rights. The " purification of the rolls "

was to them a matter of the utmost urgency; it was, literally and unequivocally, a religious duty.   Other Greeks, or
foreigners not Greek, might be permitted to settle, and trade
among them, but such persons were not partners, and they
could neither vote nor buy a house or an inch of land in Attica.
But among the Athenians themselves their system may be
summed up in the phrase "one man one vote and a perpetual
referendum."

The question will naturally occur : how then did a citizen,
man, woman, or child, become a citizen ?

The vast majority became so by birth.   They were
descendants of the citizens before them.   At some time in
antiquity the inhabitants of Attica had worked themselves into
an organised body, and its members, of all ranks, had gradually
struggled into an equality of rights.   Thenceforward all
persons born of a citizen husband and a citizen wife were
citizens.   All persons not so born were outside the pale—unless,
in exceptional cases, the whole body politic chose to bring
them inside by adopting them.   A resident foreigner could not
take out papers of naturalisation as with us.   If he lived in
the country a hundred years he could get no nearer thereby.
He might be a Rothschild; it was all the same.   Nevertheless,
the sovereign people was liberal on occasion, because, on
occasion, it was grateful.   The Outlander who had served the
country conspicuously in time of war, or who had been its
conspicuous benefactor in any other way; even the slave who
had rendered remarkable service at some critical moment; these
might be taken into the fold and made citizens, and their
children for ever after ranked as freeborn Athenians.   But this

honour was never conferred lightly. The public Assembly must first vote to bestow this privilege, then it must be re-bestowed at another Assembly, at which not less than 6000 citizens had voted; and then an inquiry might be held, and commonly was held, into claims and character, before the sanction was beyond recall.

But in the immense majority of instances the full citizen must be the child of a citizen husband and a citizen wife, who had not only been married, but had been married with all the regular formalities of betrothal and "giving away."

The child of such a marriage was, in his early infancy, entered with certain ceremonies on a register, — the register of one of those semi-religious "clans" into which all Athenians were officially divided; his full Athenian legitimacy was inquired into, and was solemnly sworn to by the father. This we may regard as a sort of certificate of baptism. One would think all this to be quite enough; nevertheless, when the young man came of age in his eighteenth year, and presented himself to be placed on the adult citizen-roll of one of those local divisions or "demes" of Attica, among which again all adult citizens were officially distributed, another strict exami-nation of his claims to citizenship could be, and theoretically must be, instituted. This stage in his career corresponds in some degree to what we should call "putting his name on the rolls" of some electoral district, although, be it remembered, the Athenian districts were not electoral in our sense, inasmuch as their parliament consisted of all citizens, and not of a body of representatives.

Suppose him, at the age of eighteen, to have satisfied the last scrutiny. He is then a complete and responsible citizen.

He can marry, bring actions at law, and, if he has been an orphan or a ward, he can now enter upon his inheritance. He will, it is true, have to serve for the next two years in the garrison and frontier militia; but, when he is free from that amount of conscription, he can settle down to his work or his leisure at Athens or in the country, and, being now twenty years of age, he can attend the Assembly and vote on an equality with Pericles or Plato. Until he is thirty, it will be bad form, though in no way illegal, for him to offer to mount the platform, at least until his seniors have said their say; also, until he is thirty, he cannot sit as a juryman in those great law-courts of which we shall have hereafter to speak. But, when he is thirty, he may be as much of an orator and a leader as his abilities can effect.

A citizen, then, has to satisfy all these conditions and all these tests. Nevertheless, in actual practice there must have been at times — but only at times — a considerable amount of laxity. There can be little doubt that occasionally money did its insidious work; also in bustling times of war and national need the scrutineers were not too particular; they found it politic to wink at irregularities; and so it came about that there was at such times a good deal of foisting on the rolls, which made it necessary for purgations and inquiries to be sometimes ordered by the Assembly. It is a common taunt of the comedians and orators that So-and-So has really no business to call himself a citizen, being only half-bred, or an alien who has got upon the rolls surreptitiously. We need not by any means believe this of any man of whom Aristophanes happens to say it; nevertheless the charge shows that such things were done, and not rarely.

F

One other point must be noted. It did not follow that, once a citizen, you were always a citizen. The state was a partnership for mutual good. The Athenians did not believe in the professional criminal, or any great offender, being treated as a partner in a healthy concern. If you were guilty of public treachery, of embezzling public money, of bribing or receiving bribes in connection with public affairs, of shirking military service or deserting your post, of perjury, of exceedingly loose living, or of insulting a magistrate in his official capacity, then you were degraded and disfranchised. You could not speak in the Assembly, nor hold any office, nor take part in public sacrifice; you could not bring an action at law, except through a proxy; you could not even appear in the Agora or public square. To reinstate you was a matter of the greatest difficulty, and exceedingly dangerous for him who proposed it.

On the other hand, if you had done anything remarkable to benefit or glorify your state, you might receive special privileges, such as exemption from certain public burdens, a front seat at all public gatherings, or free board (without lodging) in the City-hall. This was the nearest approach the Athenians made to the modern conferring of titles and pensions.

Here a question naturally suggests itself. If only Athenian citizens could attend the Assembly and vote, and if Athenian citizens included all classes of persons, even of the very poorest, and if thousands of them went up to the Pnyx to the Assembly, what was to prevent an alien or a slave or one disfranchised from slipping in and voting? The answer is easy. The Athenian community was so small, its life was so public and sociable, and the meanest labourer so jealous of his political privileges, that any intruder would certainly have been recognised and denounced to the officers or scrutineers specially appointed; the police, who were public slaves, would have seized him; and the penalty would have been so dire that the game could never be worth the candle.

Such was the first class of the Athenian population, the only class with which we propose to deal, except incidentally, in the succeeding matter. The other two classes are the resident foreigners and the slaves. Athenian society, says Aristophanes, consists of the flour, the bran, and the chaff. The flour is the citizens, the bran is the Outlanders, the chaff is the slaves.

There is one interesting point of political or social distinction which we must not forget to mention. If we saw a citizen, an Outlander, and a slave, standing side by side, and if we could not otherwise distinguish their status, it would become manifest as soon as we learned the full name by which each of the three was styled. The citizen would be named, let us say, "Demosthenes the son of Demosthenes of Paiania"; which is as though one said "Thomas Thomasson of Paddington." He has a name of his own, of his father, and of his district of registration. But a slave has no such thing as a father, and no registered district. He is called simply, let us say, Xanthias or Pyrrhias, which is much as if we named him "Redhead"; or, if he comes from a particular country, he may be given a name common in that country, as if he were called "John," "Sandy," "Pat," or "Taffy," as coming respectively from England, Scotland, Ireland, or Wales; or again, he may be ironically styled after a famous king or hero of that country, for example "Midas" if he comes from Phrygia, which is very much as if we had a

French servant and called him "Napoleon," or a Chinese servant and called him "Confucius"; or, lastly, he may be named from his country itself, such as "Thracian" or "Syrian," as though we called a servant from Holland "Dutchy" or one from Scotland "Scotty."

The Outlander, probably a foreign merchant, would be known by his own name, say, "Cephalus"; with the addition of his own country, e.g. "of Syracuse," and a statement of the Athenian district in which he lived, although he could not be registered as of it, e.g. "living in Peiraeus." We thus get "Cephalus, Syracusan, living in Peiraeus." Had he been an Athenian citizen, his style would have been "Cephalus, son of Lysias, of Peiraeus."

A final word concerning the aliens, or Outlanders, before we proceed to the slaves.

Athens, the most populous city in Greece, and a great commercial centre, naturally attracted numbers of merchants and agents from other Greek states, from Asia Minor, and from Syria. They migrated to Athens, and especially to the harbour-town of Peiraeus, almost precisely as German and other foreign merchants descend upon London or New York. Having no part whatever in politics or administration, they could devote themselves entirely to business, they were often rich, and were otherwise useful elements in society, though often looked upon askance. But they had no vote, could acquire no real property in Attica, and could not with strict legality contract marriage with an Athenian; moreover, they could not bring actions at law except through some Athenian citizen. Imagine yourself to be a French merchant migrating to London, and imagine the Athenian rules to apply to you. In the first place, after a legally specified term of residence, you must select some full citizen as your patron or guardian. In all your dealings with the administration or the courts, you must approach them and be introduced through that guardian. You are in a sense his ward. If you fail to select such a patron, you at once become liable to prosecution for being without a visible justifier of your existence. In the next place you must pay all the taxes, and also a special annual poll-tax for the right of being protected and made comfortable by the state. You must also pay a fee for permission to ply your business in the market-place. You may be called upon to perform military service in the infantry, but from the cavalry you will be excluded, and therefore you cannot go jingling your spurs along the Agora and wearing long cavalier ringlets after the manner of the choicest bloods of Athens. You may also be called to pull your oar in the warships along with the citizens. At the great Panathenaic festival you and your women-folk will be required to walk in a certain part of the procession in festal attire. If you render some considerable service to the community you may be relieved of the poll-tax, and put generally on a level with the citizens, except for the franchise. If your service has been specially signal, you may even be adopted as a full citizen. But that is rare.

Of adults in this position at Athens there were roughly about 10,000 ; and yet Athens prided itself hugely and justly on its liberality to strangers, as compared with other Greek states, such as the austere and depressing Sparta.

And now we come to the slaves. Here it would be well to

make an effort to clear our minds of certain almost inevitable false associations. The word "slave" is tolerably sure to conjure up notions of the poor negro — Uncle Tom or Sambo — and of brutal treatment by Legree and his like. We must do our best to get rid of that picture. We are now in pagan Athens, not in a modern civilisation alleged to be Christian. The Greek slave was felt to be nearer in common humanity to his master, if for no other reason, for the reason that the greatest racial repellent — difference of colour — was wanting. The Greek slave was commonly a white man : he was a servant, in the unhappy and indefensible position of compulsory, not free, servantship. His master bought him and owned him, as one might a horse; but that must not lead us to the false inferences which are too commonly drawn. A man who owns a horse may treat it well; he may even love it well; and the more used he is to owning horses the more likely he is to give it consideration. There were among the Greeks bad-tempered and heartless masters as well as kind and considerate masters; but we may repeat the analogue of the horse, and say that, from the lowest point of view, it was a master's interest to feed his slaves well, to keep them in good condition, and to see that they were properly treated when sick. Thus mutual confidences and even affection were wont to grow with time. Apart from absence of colour, the democratic sentiment of the Athenian brought him nearer to his slaves, placed him more upon terms with them, than was the case among the aristocratic planters of Old Virginia, and still more among the vulgarly pompous aristocracy which dominated imperial Rome. This is not entering any plea for slavery; above all things we must not indulge in any special pleading for the Athenians; but it is beyond dispute that the Athenian treatment of slaves compares most favourably with their treatment in any part of the ancient world, a world in which slavery was universal. The only people whose humanity to slaves probably exceeded even that of the Athenians were the Jews.

The Roman noble was commonly a proud and arrogant person. The Athenian gentleman had too much good taste and too keen a sense of humour, and was generally too clubbable, to be always posing on his dignity. Plutarch relates that a Roman master had bidden his slaves not to speak to him unless they were asked a question. He sent a slave to invite Clodius to dinner. The guests arrived, except Clodius. The master sent the slave again, to see if Clodius was coming. At last he asked, " Did you take the invitation ? " " I did, sir." " Then why does he not come ? " " Because he refused, sir." " And why did you not tell me ? " " Because you did not ask me, sir." And Plutarch goes on to compare this with the Athenian slave " who will talk to his master and discuss the news while he is digging."

The Athenian domestic slave was commonly treated as a member of the family, a subordinate and chastisable member, it is true, but a member of the family. When he or she was bought and brought home, the newcomer was welcomed by the householder with a shower of confetti. He had his share in the domestic sacrifices. He wore, as has been already observed, no distinguishing dress. When he was sick, he was looked after by the mistress. Plato tells us that only an ill-bred man would abuse his slaves, and Xenophon remarks that, unlike the slave at Sparta, the Athenian slave does not cringe nor cross the street when he meets a freeman. A master might beat his own slave, but no other citizen dare in any way injure or abuse him. Even his master could not put him to death — as the Roman could — without judicial sanction. If a master proved intolerably cruel, the slave could run to the temple of Theseus or to some altar, and there take sanctuary, demanding, not indeed his freedom, but to be sold to some one else; and the master was compelled, at least by public opinion, to grant the request.

It has seemed necessary to put these observations first, because of the horror in which we have come to regard the whole institution of slavery. It is so hard to see the better side of that which we detest as a whole. There are those who avow their conviction, after long habituation to the Attic atmosphere and to this of ours, that, despite the slaps and whippings which he too often administered, the average Athenian master stood on a footing which was at least as humane as that of the modern factory-owner, who employs by the day what he calls "hands" and who gets rid of them as soon as they are sick.

Thus much said in preface, we may for a few moments consider the practice of Athenian slavery.

It is a strange puzzle that a people so ardent for personal freedom as were the Athenians, a people who valued above all things liberty and freedom of speech, should nevertheless see nothing wrong or unreasonable in slavery. That they did not, is beyond all doubt. Never were there minds more free from cant and pretence than the minds of the Athenians, and particularly those of Socrates, Plato, and Aristotle. Yet not one of these declares against the institution. If they had unequivocally thought it wrong, they would unequivocally have said so.

On the contrary, they thought it part of the natural order of things. All ancient peoples had slaves. The Athenians had possessed them from time immemorial. This might perhaps be no logical defence. But Aristotle remarks, in his matter-of-fact way, that some men are born to be masters and others to obey, and that we should see this clearly enough, if nature had made the difference of their mental powers as visible as the difference of their bodies. And here steps in that everlasting disturber of true reason — national conceit. There is nothing more obtuse than national or racial pride. What the Gentiles were to the Jews, that the outer world was to the Greeks; its people were *barbaroi*, fit enough to have their own distinctions at home, but, as soon as they came in contact with the Greeks, only fit to be tools and instruments for the superior Greek intellect to work with. "A slave," says Aristotle, "is a live implement" of the higher intelligence.

Nor can we doubt that most of the slaves who came to Athens were socially and intellectually inferior. Nevertheless, there must have been plenteous cases of the reverse. We need not discuss this particular subject further; we can only say that the better minds of Greece, particularly the poets, recognised the hardship of the lot of a slave and insisted on his treatment as a human being.

Slaves came into Greece from various sources. Some, but comparatively few, were born of the slaves already existing. In the second place they were obtained by conquest in war. Once on a time it was taken as a matter of course that the conquered people were simply the property of the conqueror. In our period this was still the theory, but in practice it did not properly apply within the charmed circle of the Greek world itself.   When a Greek state conquered a Greek state, it was only in a fit of extreme exasperation that the vanquished were absolutely enslaved.   It was becoming abhorrent to Greek sentiment for Greeks to enslave Greeks. Ransom was accepted instead.   When no ransom was forthcoming, however, the inevitable must take place, and Aristotle's doctrine of superior and inferior intelligences must go to the wall.   Many Athenian slaves were therefore Greeks.   When the war was not with Greeks, but with other peoples, there were no scruples at all about enslaving.   The captives were simply sold to the highest bidder.   Most of the slaves, however, were bought from dealers, who picked them up or kidnapped them in Asia Minor, Syria, and the East, or in the Northern Balkans and round the Black Sea.   Again, children who had been exposed by their parents were the property of any one who found them and chose to bring them up.

From these various sources slaves were derived and brought to the Athenian market, where they were generally offered for sale on the first of the month.   Here a slave is set on a platform and inspected.   What are his points ?   What can he do ? What is his price ?   They were sold like horses at the horse-fair. A character in the comic poet Menander fancies that there is nothing left for him but slavery :   he says,   "I see myself already stripped and running round the ring on sale."   The prices are difficult to express in modern value ; what is called from £4 to £40 may really mean from £10 to £100.   According to Plato, a "tip-top carpenter" might fetch £20 or £24, while an engineer or architect might run as high as £400. When the tyrant Dionysius, in a temper, sold the philosopher

Plato, he fetched £80 (perhaps equal to £200). All this calculation, however, is very illusive. We shall never know exactly what a shilling piece would have bought in classical Athens. Let us be satisfied to consider that it would have purchased at the very least as much as half-a-crown does now.

When taken home the slave was, on the whole, treated tolerably well, so long as he behaved himself well. But the incorrigible idler, the thief, or the runaway, was treated with rigorous measures. He was hung up by the wrists and whipped; he was strapped to a ladder and whipped, after the old fashion of the British navy; he was put in the pillory, like Daniel Defoe; he was made to wear a collar, or iron fetters fastened from his waist to his ankles. He was made to weep, as the comic poet puts it, "tears four to the quart." The runaway was branded on the forehead, and, consequently, if he ever became a free man, he generally cultivated long hair over the brows or used a wig with a fringe.

By what Professor Mahaffy and others have rightly called the only really "stupid" practice among the Greeks, a slave, even a respectable slave, might be racked by the public executioner in order to extract evidence against his master in a court of law. Yet his master's consent was necessary to the act.

Now suppose yourself to possess a considerable number of slaves, male or female. What will you do with them? If you choose, you may use them all as domestic servants. There will be a maid to dress your wife, a handmaid or two to accompany her in the streets, housemaids, laundresses, nurses, wool-workers, and the like. There will be a doorkeeper, footmen and waiters, a cook and his staff, an austere attendant for the boys, and so on. You must not, it is true, have too many lackeys to attend you when you walk in the streets; two are the ideal gentleman's number; if you take three or four, you are obviously a pretentious parvenu.

If you decide for fewer domestic servants, and, therefore, as Aristotle drily observes, "for better attendance," you can put some of your slaves on your country estate as farm-labourers and grooms and gardeners. If you have still too many, or if you have no country estate, you will perhaps employ them in a factory, making one of them the manager. The father of Demosthenes manufactured swords and had fifty slaves. Or if you do not care to establish a factory in person, you can let a number of slaves establish it themselves on the co-operative system, to keep themselves and make their own profits, so long as they each pay you a few pence a day. Or, again, you may let them out to somebody else, at so much per head per day. Nicias had 1000 slaves whom he thus hired out to the lessees of the mines in Thrace.

But how many Athenians of our period, do we imagine, possessed any large number of slaves? Beyond all doubt, very few. Says Aristophanes, "One man has broad lands to farm, and another not so much as a place to be buried in. One uses a number of slaves, another has not so much as a footboy." We must firmly grasp this simple fact. By no means every Athenian possessed even a single slave. The rich Nicias may have owned 1000, and Demosthenes 50, others half-a-dozen, three, or only one. It all depended on their circumstances. A very large proportion had no notion of owning one at all.

It was, in fact, with the Athenians very much as it is with the modern household. Some keep an army of servants, some two, some one, most people none. There was also the shabby genteel lady, who, not having a maid to walk with her in the street, hired one as required for appearance sake. The majority of moderns are from poverty compelled to make their own living and to do their own work; at Athens, if not the great majority, certainly a large proportion, of the free burgesses were compelled to dispense with a slave and to accept hard and even menial work for their portion. In some cases they even let themselves out to service and performed for hire the duties which slaves performed under compulsion.

It must be mentioned also that the state too had its public slaves. These included the routine clerks in public offices, the public executioner, and the police. The police of Athens were Scythians, armed with a bow, and it is curious to find Aristophanes making the Scythian policemen talk their Attic Greek with a very pronounced brogue. Their function was to keep order at the public meetings, to attend the magistrates, and to carry out magisterial instructions. But they had no regular beats and did not patrol the city. Perhaps it may be of interest to know that this body of 1200 men, having been first suggested by a certain Speusinos, were colloquially styled " Speusinioi," just as the English police were dubbed "Peelers" and "Bobbies" after their father Sir Robert Peel. This is only one of a thousand small points in which history curiously repeats itself.

Finally, the slave might be set free by his master; he might purchase his own freedom; or, for some extraordinary service, the state might buy him from his master and make him into a citizen. When this was done, the act and the name were cried by the public crier in the theatre or at other public rendezvous, so that there might be no mistake thereafter. This was one Athenian way of what we should call "announcing in the newspapers" or "gazetting."

We now return to our citizens. It should perhaps by this time have become sufficiently clear that in pecuniary and social position the Athenians were anything but on an equality. Many possessed landed estates, many were farmers with small ones, some owned factories, some were merchants or shipowners, many were simple shopkeepers, artisans, seamen, peasants, even day-labourers and hucksters in the market. The father of Demosthenes was a sword manufacturer; the mother of Euripides, if we may believe the comedians, was a greengrocer. Plutarch, speaking of Pericles and the great buildings executed by the democracy under his guidance, asserts that one of Pericles' motives was to supply work. These works would "stir up every craft, set every hand at work, and make practically all the state wage-earners. As he did not wish the vulgar populace either to go without their share, or to receive it without doing any work, he threw before the people proposals for great structures, and projects calling for numerous arts and crafts, requiring time to complete them. . . . The material required was stone, bronze, ivory, gold, ebony, cypress wood; the crafts dealing with it included carpenters, modellers, smiths, stonemasons, dyers, moulders of gold and ivory, painters, embroiderers and workers in relief; persons were needed to bring these things; if by way of the sea, merchants, sailors, and pilots; if by land, cartwrights, team-breeders, drivers, rope-makers, linen-makers, shoemakers, roadmakers, and miners. Each trade, moreover, had its own army of unskilled labourers, acting as tools. In fact, there was a demand for persons of every age and capacity." Now these men were citizens : neither Pericles nor the democracy were concerned with the providing of work for slaves.

Nevertheless, it may be asked, did not the Athenians as a rule despise work and trade ? The answer is both Yes and No. The employment of slaves had made work unnecessary for some classes, and these classes pitied those to whom work was necessary. That is human nature. It followed in Athens, as anywhere else, that some human beings were better dressed, had cleaner persons, and enjoyed leisure for more mental and social cultivation than others. The inevitable result was an obvious outward advantage of those who did not perform manual labour over those who did. And no people in the world ever set such a value on outward superiority of person and manners as did the classical Athenians. We must be frank on this point. In the first place, they did not despise work as such, nor were they constitutionally indolent; what they disliked was the uncomely physical effects of labour, especially of indoor labour; they detested that which made them acquire a stoop or stunted the limbs, or misshaped the hands, or begrimed the person. In the second place, they had an intense passion for personal independence, and their ideal of personal freedom of action and speech could hardly be attained by one who had to serve and court the custom of his neighbour. In the third place, the vulgar and material concerns of the lower occupations prevent the mind from gathering the culture and refinement which come of good company and abundance of intellectual intercourse.

There is perhaps, after all, a good deal of solid fact at the bottom of this attitude. But whereas we try to make the best of the inevitable, and leave it to the snobs to despise the worker, the Athenians were made the more impatient with it because they had come to regard the unpleasantness of life as a part proper for slaves.   Hence, toward the end of our period, when the state treasury was generally fairly full, as many citizens as possible endeavoured to get rid of manual labour and to live, however frugally, on payments from the state — fees for attending the Assembly, fees for jury service, for military service, or fees for great or small offices.   In modern times this would mean that they tried to become members of parliament and civil servants of the order which weareth a black coat.   But, then as now, they could not all be in the public service at once ; manual work many did and must do.

Practically, then, manual labour at least was disliked.   But theoretically the better minds of Athens never despised either work or poverty.   Certain special occupations, it is true, were held in frank contempt.   Says Theophrastus concerning the Reckless or Unscrupulous Man : " He is the sort of person to become an inn-keeper, or a tax-farmer ; he will decline no sort of unseemly occupation, but will act as a public crier or as cook." An ancient inn was not like a modern inn, and in the occupations named, as they were prosecuted in antiquity, the citizen must bring himself into humiliating or impudent situations.   Such occupations as these were for that reason openly despised.

But there is this to be said of classical Athens.   There was no titled aristocracy, and there was very little of the social ostentation which characterises the " wealthy lower orders " of modern times.   There was, at this date, little of that vulgar running after rich people which is the most deplorable feature of our own day.   In Athenian society, therefore, the question of your standing depended much more than with us, and infinitely more than at Rome, on your social qualifications and refinement. Socrates was not worth twenty pounds in the world; but he possessed a splendid intellect and much social humour, and he could dine when he chose with Alcibiades and Callias and the rest of the *élite*. Similarly Plutarch remarks of one person that " he was a shoemaker, but he was a familiar figure in the wrestling-schools and enjoyed a wide acquaintance."   If a man could be an artisan and yet prove that he was cultivated and personally acceptable, he had little to complain of in the matter of social recognition.

Unfortunately such cases were necessarily few.   The Athenian state was democratic; but if we are asked whether Athenian society was equally democratic, we must make that answer.   Your ultimate social criterion was rather what you were, than what you did.   It was not, and could not be, the case that each and every citizen in whatsoever state of person and of whatsoever manners and culture was equally welcome company to Pericles and to the huckster in the market-place. There were also, doubtless, snobs and toadies, but in our period they were almost professionally such, and probably the Athenian idea of society was on the whole the most rational hitherto invented or developed.

But what of the women? We shall here deal only with their status, not with their private life, which belongs to a later discussion. It is a great blot on Athenian civilisation that the position of woman had retrograded since the days of Homer. Her business now is simply to be the housewife and housemother, to apportion to the slaves their domestic work,

G

to regulate the stores, to weave and superintend the weaving of garments, and to bring up the girls and little boys. She has received no particular education beyond these domestic accomplishments. Her place is inside the house. She may go abroad at festivals and on other recognised occasions, if properly attended, but the best woman, according to the Athenian definition, is she of whom "least is said for either good or harm."

There you have, as succinctly as one can put it, the accepted theory of Athenian marriage. In this respect the Athenians were far less liberal than Sparta and other Grecian states. One may be inclined to think that there was something racial in this. In the Ionian Greeks, including the Athenians, there was a much larger proportion of the earlier pre-Hellenic or Mediterranean stock than in the other branches of the Greek world. We may imagine that this fact told in the treatment of women. Again, it is hardly fair to compare Athens with Homeric Greece. Homeric Greece scarcely possessed cities, whereas the close and crowded city life and narrow streets of Athens rendered a certain seclusion more necessary for women. And, lastly, the Ionian Greeks had certainly learned from the luxurious Asiatics a portion of their social rules of good form; and since it was good form to seclude women in Asia Minor, it became good form to seclude them in Ionian Greece. When this practice of seclusion had become general and had been established for generations, it necessarily followed that women grew more and more ignorant of the world, and became intellectually, as they were physically, inferior. What more natural than for men then to treat them as if their ignorance and inferiority were natural rather than acquired?

Be this as it may, the fact remains that it was in the greatest age of Athens that women were least important. To a man public life, or at least life in public, was everything; his home life hardly counted. He married generally a girl much younger than himself, not because he cared for her — perhaps he had scarcely, if ever, seen her — but because there was a public and social duty in marriage. A *mariage de convenance*, often arranged by a professional matchmaker, was the commonest form. To an Athenian marriage was apt to be irksome: "What!" says one character in a comedy, "Married! Did you say he was married? Why it was only the other day I saw him alive and walking about."

An Athenian might marry any citizen woman, except in the direct line of his own descent. He could even marry — though he rarely did — his half-sister on the father's side. But the woman whom he married, probably when she was sixteen or eighteen, never passed into the full power of her husband. She was by law connected all the time more closely with her own family than with his. At no time of her life could a woman be without a guardian. If her father was not alive, it would be her nearest male relative, and this person remained her guardian even when she was married. After her husband's death her son was her guardian. She could not legally make any contract beyond a shilling or two — there was no occasion for an Athenian to advertise that he would not be responsible for his wife's debts — and she could not bring actions at law. A dowry played the same part as in France; it was practically essential. But at Athens the dowry never became the husband's property. If it took the form of money, he must give security for it. On the other hand, the husband's property never became the wife's. She had no claim upon it when he was dead.

For the man divorce was easy. Legally, he had simply to hand back the dowry, ask his wife to give up the keys, and bid her return home. On the other side it was exceedingly difficult, though by no means impossible, for the woman to obtain a divorce.

It is sometimes stated that at Athens there was a board of officers appointed to keep a general control over the comings and goings of women and over their good behaviour. But certainly no such board existed in our period, and Aristotle observes that such officers — who did exist elsewhere in Greece — would be an undemocratic institution ; " for how," says he, " can you prevent the poor from going out, when the wives and daughters are obliged to do what slaves perform in other families ? "

It is perhaps as well to remark here, so as not to leave any false impression until we deal more fully with the women, that the theory was much more strict than the practice. There was a good deal of natural affection ; there was in reality a good deal of freedom. The very prominence which is given to women in the comedies and elsewhere shows their real influence. Solon had to legislate that " anything done under the influence of woman should be illegal." " Sir," said Dr. Johnson, " Nature has given woman so much power that the law cannot afford to give her any more." That natural power existed at Athens as much as anywhere else. Sophocles and Euripides could not have drawn such types of noble and commanding women unless they had actually met with something of the kind. What should we say if we knew that, twenty centuries hence, some one would take hold of the words in the English Prayer-Book, " Love, honour and obey," as a proof that the modern wife had no will of her own ?   In a play of Aristophanes the wife says, " When I asked my husband, ' What did the Assembly decide about the negotiations for peace ? ' he replied, ' What has that to do with you ?   Stop talking,' " and then she adds, somewhat unbelievably, " and I stopped talking."   But, on the other hand, one hears Demosthenes describe a man discussing politics with his wife at dinner.   For the present, let it suffice to say that the position of the Athenian woman was in practice more free and agreeable than it seems in theory.

CHAPTER V

HOUSE AND FURNITURE

CHAPTER V

HOUSE AND FURNITURE

HAVING dealt with the several classes of the population, and having decided to restrict ourselves henceforth to the citizens proper, let us now proceed to look at the house in which such a citizen might dwell, and the sort of furniture with which he would surround himself.

It is of course obvious that, if we describe a house, it must be simply a typical house of the representative class, the house of a free Athenian citizen of average manners and cultivation and of average means. And if we repeat that there were humble houses, houses partly workshop or selling-shop and partly dwelling-house, often, moreover, mere cells, smoky and squalid and overcrowded, we shall have sufficiently safeguarded the truth, so far as is necessary for the general sketch which we are here making of Athenian life.

Here we have nothing to do with the ancient Homeric so-called "palace," nor yet with the later spacious and luxurious mansions of Graeco-Roman times. It was only at the very close of our chosen period, when truly democratic public life was coming to an end under the dominion of Macedonia, that more sumptuous abodes began to be erected at Athens. Says Demosthenes at that time: "if any of you know what the house of Themistocles, of Miltiades, and of the distinguished men of those days was like, you know that it made no more show than the general run of houses, whereas the public buildings were such as no subsequent edifice could ever transcend. . . . But nowadays the public men are all so affluent that some of them have built their own houses to make more show than the public buildings." This, of course, was a rhetorical exaggeration, but it illustrates our point.

In the city proper, large houses were in any case out of the question. The country houses were more roomy and were preferred by Athenians who possessed both; Athenian families loved to escape to them. If anything like a spacious house was to be built at Athens, it had to be in the suburbs. In this respect, of course, history manifestly repeats itself.

If now we take our typical house, it must be understood that it is but typical, and that, as with us, all sorts of arrangements of rooms were possible. There were, for example, houses of one storey, houses of two storeys, and houses with an upper storey only half covering the lower.

But of almost all houses alike, in the city itself, it may be said that we of this age, after making ourselves familiar with the temples and porticoes, could not fail to be surprised and disappointed at the common-looking exterior and the paltry-sized apartments of the private dwellings. It was not that the Athenian was insensible to private architecture, nor that he would naturally have disapproved of large and imposing dwellings; but the city began by being poor, there was no room to spare, there was a generally democratic sentiment against individual display, and, most of all, the house was not, at this time, regarded by the lord and master with the feeling with which we regard a home. He lived so much in the open, and was so much occupied in public and private business and in meeting his friends in the gymnasia and colonnades of the city, that his domicile was little more than a place in which to sleep, to house his secluded family, and occasionally to give a dinner-party to a few male friends.

Truth to tell, our information concerning the Athenian house is not so satisfactory as concerning some other matters. Nevertheless, some ground-plans have been laid bare in the Peiraeus, and we have a certain number of partial and rather obscure descriptions and a large number of scattered notes. We must not take the ruins of Pompeii as irrefragable evidence. Pompeii was a Roman watering-place, no doubt built under much Greek influence; but it was not true Greek; it was in Italy; it was not Athens; and we are speaking of a period four centuries at least before the destruction of Pompeii. We can only say that, in default of anything better, Pompeii would be of much help in forming an impression of the comparative smallness of Athenian houses and Athenian rooms, and also of the general principle of arrangement.

The chief principle in respect of which the Athenian house differed most widely from ours was this — that it was built round one or more open courts, and that the light and air were obtained from inside from these courts, and not, as with us, from large and numerous windows. We may sum up the situation by saying that there was more privacy from outside, less privacy inside.

The front of a one-storied house toward the street was practically a blank wall. It might show one or two narrow slits or lattices at nine or ten feet from the ground, but not necessarily even these. A two-storied house would generally have somewhat larger lattices overlooking the street on the upper floor, and that upper floor often overhung the street. Covered with stucco, or simply whitewashed, or tinted in monochrome, the front would rank with us as virtually a blank wall. To the curiosity of the outside world it was entirely closed. But when you stood in the enclosed court, you could look round upon practically every room, and to pass from one room to another except by way of the court was generally impossible.

This appears the right place to remark that into the walls of many of the larger houses a shop or shops might be inserted, much as they are inserted from the street into the structure of our modern large hotels. The shop seldom belonged to the householder, but was generally let. Sometimes it was entered by the actual doorway of the house.

The walls themselves, that is to say, the actual structure of the house, consisted sometimes of a framework of wood covered with stucco, sometimes of common stone, but generally of bricks, which were only sun-dried, not baked in a kiln, and were therefore liable to crumble away or to be easily broken down. That, indeed, is one of the reasons why our knowledge cannot be assisted in Greece by much in the way of actual remains of walls. For the same reason, if a Greek burglar desired to break into a house, he commonly did so by digging a hole through the wall, and the Greek for burglar is consequently " wall-digger." Later, no doubt, there were houses of marble or other stone; but our period and our typical house are not concerned with these materials.

It is not to be supposed that Athenian houses were all alike, whether in dimensions or arrangement. There did not, it is true, exist the extremes which mark a later period or the present day; yet the situation of a building, and the circumstances of the family, naturally determined the number, size, and disposition of the rooms. We must be satisfied with as near a picture as we can get of the house of a fairly well-to-do citizen of our epoch. It will be well first to take a glance at the plan before us.

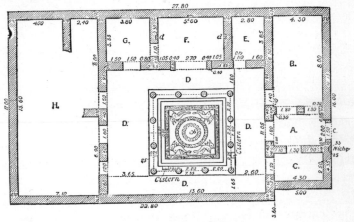

Fig. 14. — House at Delos.

This is the ground-plan of a house at Delos found by the French excavators in the island. A front door opens into a passage (A), beside which is a cell (C), probably for the porter. This passage leads into a court (D), with cloisters round, and a mosaic floor in the midst; off the court are rooms (E, F, G), with a larger space behind (H), the arrangements of which are doubtful.

This plan is more to be trusted than the speculative schemes which are to be found in handbooks and dictionaries of antiquities. It is of the second century B.C. The building probably had an upper storey : it is evident that in a house of this kind space for the women's rooms might be found either on a second floor or in the area (H). It is unlikely that houses at Athens in the fourth century were more elaborate than this at Delos.

Allowing thus for considerable difference of detail, we may now assume that we are paying a visit to the town house of our citizen.

In older times railings were now and then to be met with, but in our period these, as well as steps encroaching on the

Fig. 15. — Vestibule; conjectural view.

street, were forbidden. The richer home might have its vestibule or porch, and a step or two might mount to the door proper inside that space, but such a vestibule did not project so as to block any portion of the street. In front of the house stood an emblem of Hermes and of "Apollo of the streets."

The Hermes was regularly a bearded bust upon a squared pillar of stone; the Apollo was frequently a mere conical post serving as symbol. Occasionally, where there was a vestibule, a laurel-tree stood by the Apollo. The door itself formerly opened outward, but the danger and inconvenience of this were obvious, and the practice was now prohibited. The

double leaves of which the door was regularly composed may
be seen in the illustration, p. 96. The hinges upon which these
opened were vertical pivots running into the threshold and

FIG. 16. — Decorating a Hermes.

the lintel, and the opening of a door was apt to be noisy, unless the pivots were oiled, or, if made of wood, watered. On
one leaf is a knocker, consisting commonly of the ring in a

lion's mouth which has survived in so many places till this day.

The original purpose of the lion's head was to scare away evil influences, and, in keeping with this notion, it was usual to place over the door an inscription, the favourite being "Let no evil enter here." This practice lent itself to the quips of the sarcastic, and we are told of retorts such as "But how is the owner to get in?"

On hearing the knock at the door, the porter issues from his lodge (C) and opens to scrutinise the visitor. Sometimes the

FIG. 17.—Door (in interior).

door is already open, but this is unusual. While waiting for an answer to his knock, the visitor may perhaps be contemplating the legend, "Beware of the dog." The porter, who is of course a slave, is for the most part not distinguished by amiability. He is a person of some trust and discretion, since it is his business to watch all comings and goings, both of the free occupants and the slaves, and also to see what is brought in and carried out. He serves as buffer against the outer world to a domestic life which was jealous of observation. The Greeks, says Plutarch at a later date, had "knockers to rattle on the doors so that the stranger might not catch the mistress in the open, nor the unmarried daughter, nor a slave being chastised, nor the servant-girls screaming." The porter is therefore an important personage, and he has little scruple in snapping out "not at home," or even slamming the door in one's face. But to a welcome friend the porter, we are told, was all smiles and his dog all waggings of the tail; and by such indications a visitor might gauge his footing in the house.

The porter has admitted us into the passage (A), — in the floor of which is probably inlaid the word " welcome " — and thence leads us into the main court (D), which, when there are two in the house, is conveniently to be distinguished as the "men's court." Round the four sides of a space open to the sky runs a covered colonnade, of which the roof is supported on perhaps a dozen pillars of about ten feet in height. Under this cover seats may be placed, or a constitutional walk may be taken. In the open middle stands the domestic altar, dedicated to " Zeus of the Home," at which the housefather will on occasion officiate amid the family and the slaves. The floor, at our period, is made of concrete, varied with simple patterns, but without any of that elaborate mosaic work which came in at a later date from Pergamus. To either hand there open off a number of rooms (E, etc.), most of which we should rather regard as cells. Whether these were provided with doors or portières or both, was apparently a matter which depended on their use and on the tastes of the household. The smallest of them are sleeping-rooms for males, whether slaves or visitors, and such a room may be put down as being of not more than one-third of the size which we should regard as adequate. Somewhere, however, there is necessarily an apartment of considerable size to be used as the dining-room for the male parties, which are frequently given and which we are later to describe. It is the court itself which is commonly

H

used as reception-room, sitting-room, and place for the family meals. "My wife," observes one litigant in Demosthenes, "was lunching with the children in the court." Tame birds or other animals are also not uncommon in it.

And here nothing could be better than to quote from the *Protagoras* of Plato a passage which will excellently illustrate what has been so far said. Socrates and Hippocrates visit the wealthy Callias, who is entertaining distinguished professors. "We proceeded on our way until we reached the vestibule of the house; and there we stopped, in order to conclude a dispute which had arisen as we were going along; and we stood talking in the vestibule until we had finished. And I think that the doorkeeper, who was probably annoyed at the great inroad of the Sophists, must have heard us talking. At any rate, when we knocked at the door, and he opened and saw us, he grumbled: 'They are Sophists — he is not at home,' and instantly gave the door a hearty bang with both hands. Again we knocked, and he answered without opening: 'Did you not hear me say that he is not at home, fellows?' 'But, my friend,' said I, 'you need not be alarmed; for we are not Sophists, and we are not come to see Callias, but we want to see Protagoras; and I must request you to announce us.' At last, after a good deal of difficulty, the man was persuaded to open the door.

"When we entered we found Protagoras taking a walk in the portico. . . . A train of listeners followed him. . . . Nothing delighted me more than the precision of their movements; they never got into his way at all; but when he and those who were with him turned back, then the band of listeners parted regularly on either side; he was always in front, and they wheeled round and took their places behind him in perfect order. After him, as Homer says, 'I lifted up my eyes and saw' Hippias the Elean sitting in the opposite portico on a chair of state, and around him were seated on benches Eryximachus and others; they were putting to Hippias certain physical and astronomical questions, and he, *ex cathedra*, was determining their several questions to them. Also 'my eyes beheld' Prodicus: he had been lodged in a room which had been a storeroom; but, as the house was full, Callias had cleared this out and made the room into a guest-chamber. Now Prodicus was still in bed, wrapped up in sheepskins and bedclothes . . . and there were sitting by him on the couches near, Pausanias and others."

Separating the reception rooms, or men's quarters, from the more private apartments, or women's quarters, there is an intermediate door. Through this door strangers are not admitted, and, in the stricter households, the unmarried daughters do not come from beyond it, unless with special reason and permission. It was, of course, a heinous social offence to act like the accused in a speech of Demosthenes : "He came to my house one night intoxicated, broke the doors open, and entered the women's quarters!"

In this more secluded part of the house are the bed-chambers of the master and mistress and of the unmarried daughters. There are also the storeroom, rooms for the handmaidens to work and sleep in, a kitchen, and other offices. Behind all these there is sometimes a garden with a door leading into it.

So far it has been assumed that the house is of but one storey. But in the city, where ground-space was so limited, a second floor was generally indispensable. This might extend over the whole area of the lower rooms, in which case it frequently overhung the streets, as in many old English towns, or it covered but a portion, and so formed what was called a "tower." There appears to have been no rule as to who should occupy the upper storey, and the practice naturally differed according to the convenience of a household. Sometimes it would be the women, sometimes the slaves. Often the upper storey was let, and in such cases was approached from the street by separate stairs. Though windows were practically unknown on the lower floor, the upper might be provided

FIG. 18. — Upper lattice.

with casements looking on the street. In these there was no glass or other transparent material, but wooden doors were opened and shut. Meanwhile the roof itself was commonly flat, and so served as a vantage-ground for viewing processions and shows. In other cases, however, it was gabled, the pinnacle being known as "the eagle."

The better houses contained a cistern or even a well. The water which collected about the house was carried off by a drain into the street. Chimneys, in our sense of the word, did not exist. The fires — which were seldom necessary — consisted of wood or charcoal, carried in braziers to the place where they were needed, and the smoke found its way out as best it could. In the kitchen alone was there a fixed fireplace provided with some sort of flue. This certainly carried the smoke to a hole of outlet, which might be covered, when not required, by a board or trap-door.

Of decorative fixture there was little. Beyond the patterns in the cement floor there was scarcely anything except stucco ornaments and coloured traceries on the ceiling. In the lesson in modern manners which the son gives to the father in the *Wasps* of Aristophanes, it is enjoined that he shall "take a view of the ceiling." If the painter Agatharchus was kept a prisoner

FIG. 19. — Brazier.

in the house of Alcibiades until he had decorated it, we are nevertheless unable to say what precise shape the decorations took.

After this brief survey of the imaginary typical house, it remains to recall to mind that a portion of it (such as B) might be let or used as a shop. Also it was not uncommon for a horse or donkey to be stabled in the house, apparently close to the door and the porter's lodge.

The furniture of a classical Athenian home was very simple; it would undoubtedly be regarded by us as very scanty. In

compensation it was for the most part extremely happy in the
blending of gracefulness and utility. In what the contemporary
auctioneer might have described as an " elegantly furnished man-
sion " there was perhaps little that we should call cosey. On
the other hand, there was an absence of the plethora and welter
of things upholstered which are only too common in modern
times. There was sufficiency for real use, and the sufficiency
was rendered doubly sufficient by the satisfaction with which
the eye could always rest upon it.

Athenian chairs were of several kinds, some being without
backs and often foldable, others provided with backs but either

with or without arms. The chief types
are shown in our illustrations. None of
the chairs are upholstered, but cushions
are used when desired. The legs and flat
surfaces of the more costly chairs are
often inlaid with silver, tortoise, or ivory.
Couches also play a great part in Athenian

Fig. 20. — Chairs.

furnishing. These are either beds or sofas, the latter being
used for ordinary reclining or by the men at their dinner-
parties. Among the rich a point was made of securing
elegance of shape in the frames, whether of bronze or wood ;
and here again the flat surfaces were much inlaid and the
legs made sumptuous with silver or ivory. The bed proper
consisted of such a frame with canvas or leather thongs
stretched from side to side ; on this were laid a mattress
stuffed with flock, pillows filled with wool or feathers, and
coverlets of wool or skins, dyed with purple and other colours.
Meanwhile the poor were content with truckle-beds, or even
with mats, or canvas bags stuffed with leaves.

Tables, which were of either three or four legs, and of light and graceful structure, were scarcely in use except at meals, when they were brought in and carried out with the food. They apparently fulfilled no other of the purposes of the modern table. Even writing was done, not upon a table, but upon the right knee, which was raised for the purpose. (For the forms of couches and tables see the scenes of feasting, Chapter VII.)

A special attention was, however, spent upon the carved and inlaid chests, which served as wardrobes and plate-safes, and incidentally as seats. Athenian clothes were such that they could most conveniently be folded and laid flat, and both garments and articles of value were most easily kept by locking and sealing in a chest.

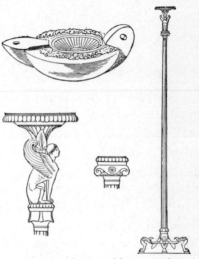

Other articles of furniture consisted of braziers, used both for warming and for the burning of perfumes ; lamps, either hanging by chains or placed upon stands ; baskets of various shapes and col-

FIG. 21. — Lamp and lamp-stand.

ours ; hand-mirrors of polished bronze, mostly circular, with reliefs worked upon the back and along the handles ; and, above all, an abundant variety of vessels in bronze, silver, and earthenware, intended mostly for use, but always for ornament.

The Greek names of different recognised species of cups, vases, and dishes make a formidable catalogue. Some few specimens only can be illustrated here and in Chapter VII. Figure 22 represents a quantity of household furniture burned by Hercules in a fit of madness, from a vase-painting.

True carpets were unknown at this date, but a few rugs and curtains were not uncommon.

Fig. 22. — Domestic furniture.

Sparing in quantity as the furniture of the Athenians was, it is certain that they had learned the secret of lending an artistic effect without destroying the use or comfort of the article. Having secured the shape which both pleased the eye and served the purpose, they sought no novelty in this domain, but were content to retain the same unimprovable types for centuries.

CHAPTER VI

THE SOCIAL DAY OF A TYPICAL CITIZEN
(TILL DINNER)

CHAPTER VI

THE SOCIAL DAY OF A TYPICAL CITIZEN (TILL DINNER)

OUR typical citizen is the adult male citizen who enjoys the leisure to dispose of his day according to his own choice. It is one of those days on which there is no meeting of the Assembly, no sitting of a court in which he is to serve as one of the great jury of five hundred, no performance in the theatre, and no religious festival. The procedure of days on which these public events take place requires separate treatment. We are here concerned only with the round of a typical full day of social life.

Incidentally we shall speak of the unleisured Athenian — the artisan or dealer or wage-earner — whenever we come across him while accompanying our friend throughout the day.

Well, our Athenian, being a man of some means, probably lives in the quarter named Collytus, or somewhere near the Cerameicus; for the several quarters of Athens were, like those of our own towns, more and less fashionable. He rises at a very early hour, somewhere about daybreak. The Athenian is no slug-a-bed, whether he be rich or poor. He would regard as unpardonably late our usual hour for catching our suburban train, and by the time our city offices are open he would have got half through the business (if he had any) and also some of the pleasure of the day. If he wishes to make a call on a friend, and to be sure of finding him at home, he will do so

107

immediately after dawn. When Hippocrates was eager to take Socrates with him to call on Professor Protagoras, who had just arrived in Athens, he came along to Socrates' house before daylight and, as Plato has it, "gave a tremendous thump on the door with his stick." He made Socrates get up from his truckle-bed, and was all impatience to start. But Socrates replies, "Not yet, my good fellow, it is too early. But let us take a turn in the court and wait about till daybreak; when the day breaks, then we will go." And here we may recall how, as described in our account of the Greek house, they found Protagoras already walking about under the verandah round the court, and how there was already a houseful of other callers.

Rising from his bed, our citizen washes his face and hands and dresses for the street.

Before we observe him and his attire as he issues from his doorway, let us remark that he breaks his fast — literally that and nothing more — by taking the first meal, if you can call it a meal, of the day. This consists of a few mouthfuls of bread dipped in neat wine. Practically it corresponds to the coffee and roll taken in France, or to the early tea and bread-and-butter common among ourselves. He will require nothing else till nearly mid-day, the time of the French *déjeuner*, or of a very early lunch. Then he will make a substantial meal; but, in the meanwhile, what our own ancestors called his "sop in wine" will suffice him; for, whatever may be his faults, he is no glutton.

His dress in this classical time is very simple, as you may perceive from any portrait statue of Sophocles or Demosthenes.

FIG. 23. — Portrait statue; Sophocles.

But it must be again premised that, despite this general
simplicity, the Athenians by no means all dressed in garments
of precisely the same number or the same material or worn in
precisely the same style or of the same colour.   It is true that

they could have made no attempt to compete with our modern fearful and wonderful diversity. Apart from the head and feet, the Athenian covered his body with two articles of attire at most, often with only one. It is also worth while noting here that astonishingly little change of fashion occurred during long centuries of Grecian history. The practical Greek had discovered what costume suited his climate, and, being artistic as well as practical, he had settled upon a costume which did justice to the scenic possibilities of the human form. As in buildings and articles of furniture, he first developed what was suitable, then rendered it artistic, and then adhered to it with an intelligent loyalty which we might well imitate, if ever we are fortunate enough to combine similarly the useful with the decorative.

The costume of a leisured Athenian would not, it is true, prove the best possible for our climate or working conditions; neither would it suit modern European notions as to the legitimate amount of revelation of the human form divine. But for a leisured man in ancient Athens, and for the very different conception which was then entertained concerning the said human form, it was perfect in its kind.

The Athenian male attire, we have said, consisted of but two articles, the tunic and the mantle. Both of these were — to put it simply — oblongs or squares of material, mostly woollen, draped round the body. If one took off the garments of which the illustrations are given, and spread them out, it would be found that they were in general nothing more nor less than such oblongs or squares. If the tunic was partly sewn to shape, that sewing was the minimum possible. Briefly stated, the ordinary full dress consisted of an under tunic and

Fig. 24. — Demosthenes.

an upper robe or mantle. But, according to the weather, or
his taste, or his occupation, or the function in which he was to
be engaged, the Athenian might wear both of those, or only
the under tunic, or only the mantle. If he wore the tunic

FIG. 25. — Tunic; statue at Delphi.

only he was said to be "in undress." If, like Socrates, he
wore only the robe, he was doing a very common thing. You
would not, as a matter of good form, address the sovereign
people in your tunic only, but you might and did in the robe

only. Such conduct was perhaps not strictly ideal, but statues indicate that it was not incorrect in practice.

The tunic worn by a man of leisure had two armholes, but no sleeves. It fell to just above the knee, and could be girdled.

A workman's tunic had only a left armhole, while the right shoulder and arm were quite free and the tunic came round underneath them. He commonly used a girdle. This freedom of the right arm, as may be seen from the illustrations, was also frequently consulted by gentlemen in their manner of wearing the robe.

In putting on the upper robe—the *himation*, as it was called — you took the long piece of cloth, threw it over your left shoulder, then brought it across the back and either over or under the right arm, as you thought fit or convenient, and then threw it again over your left shoulder

FIG. 26. — Workman's tunic; Hephaestus.

or arm. If properly adjusted, the mantle then held naturally in place, although small weights might be attached to the lower border to assist that purpose. Simple as it appears, to do this with neatness and grace was as difficult as all good draping is. The estimation of what we call the good and bad "cut" of our

clothes corresponds almost exactly to the estimation in which
the Athenians held what was simply graceful or awkward
adjustment of the long mantle. If we pause to reflect upon
that fact, we may perceive that it does the usual credit to

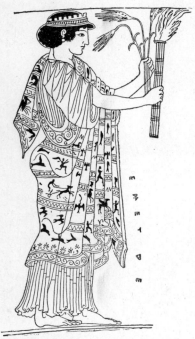

FIG. 27. — Bordered garment; Demeter.

Athenian taste and artistic
principle. Nor was it
merely necessary to make
the mantle hang well; it
must also fall to the right
length, which was to the
lower part of the shins,
over which it crossed ob-
liquely. If it fell short of
this, you were dressed like
a rustic; if it trailed on the
feet, your style was loud
and pretentious. It must
not be supposed that we
are here making too much
of details. The Athenians
themselves saw real defects
of character in either slov-
enliness or loudness. De-
mosthenes does not think
it out of place to prejudice his opponent even in a law-court
by remarking that "he marches through the Agora with his
mantle down to his ankles, striding along and puffing out his
cheeks."

In point of colour a crowd of Athenians would appear by no
means so monotonous as is usually supposed. They were not

all dressed in white.   It is true that both tunic and mantle were commonly white or nearly so, especially with staid or elderly citizens; nevertheless, colours were not rare, especially with young or fashionable men.   Purple, red, frog-green, and black were to be met with, but yellow was a colour for women only.   Even if the whole material were not coloured, it was frequently adorned with coloured borders, embroidery, or stripes, either worked in or sewn on; and not seldom fringes or tassels were added.   Doubtless when a certain Ionian came to Athens, and wore a purple cloak with gold fringe, he was considered altogether too gorgeous a being, but equally, beyond doubt, the young bloods and dandies of Athens affected a good deal of showy and expensive colour.

And here we must be reminded to say that, besides our ordinary type of modestly, but carefully, attired citizen, in his tunic and mantle (or only his mantle), you would see in the Athenian streets sundry special types, distinctly

Fig. 28. — Ephebus in *chlamys.*

attired.   There is the young man, just come of age at eighteen. For the space of two years he wears, instead of the long mantle and sandals of the older man, a hat, shoes, and a shorter and bright cloak (or *chlamys*), fastened over his shoulder by a brooch or buckle.   Of him a rough and incomplete illustration is forthcoming.   There is again the deliberate imitator of the

Spartans, often a philosopher who affects to scorn fashion and comfort.   This man wears a short rough cloak, generally from a pure spirit of ostentatious contrariety.

Artisans often wear leather jerkins.   Shepherds and peasants may come into town wearing clothing of skins with the hair or wool on them, while the very poorest of either citizens or slaves may even be seen in sacking or a sort of matwork.

Our representative citizen will in ordinary circumstances wear no covering to his head.   Nature was liberal to the

FIG. 29. — Hats and caps.

Greeks in respect of hair, and in town a head-cover was generally unnecessary and certainly unusual. An invalid might indeed use a cap, and a traveller in the country would either wear a close rimless cap or a hat with a brim, hardly differing from certain shapes of felt hats well known among us.   But one cannot imagine a Pheidias or a Plato or a Demosthenes walking in the Agora with anything but a bare head.   Slaves, and persons much exposed to the weather, such as peasants and sailors, commonly wore skull-caps, but our friend who is walking out this morning is protected only by his natural locks.

But he will, in all probability, wear something on his feet. It is not necessary that he should.   In the house he will commonly go barefoot or wear slippers; when he steps outside he will still please himself.   Much will depend on the time of year.   The streets were, as we have explained, not of the best, and both cleanliness and comfort were consulted by shoes, or at least by sandals.   Hardy men of the old school, like Socrates or Phocion, elected to walk abroad with bare feet.   Socrates preferred to do so even in winter, and many of the poor had no choice in the matter. The ostentatious philosophers who were just now mentioned as wearing short mantles, also showed their artificial hardihood by refusing shoes. Meanwhile the really hardy men, such as the peasants and soldiers, were always glad to wrap their feet in winter time in brogues of raw hide, or in felt or lambskins.

FIG. 30. — Sandal of Hermes.

The only condition really necessary to be obeyed by our typical citizen is that, if he wears shoes or sandals at all, they shall fit him properly and be put well on. He is not bound to wear them to show that he is a gentleman, but, if shod, he is bound to be shod as a gentleman ought. It is only a rustic who wears shoes too big for his feet, or as Aristophanes puts it "is swimming in his shoes."

The simplest form of foot-covering was the sandal. This consisted of a leather sole, or sometimes of two layers of leather with a layer of cork between, held to the foot by means of a strap, which passed between the great toe and the next, and was fastened to other straps running along the foot and also down to the heel. The straps might be coloured, particularly red, and an ornamental clasp might be fixed where they met on the instep. Perhaps we may remark that the Greek sandal and slipper were favourite instruments of domestic corporal punishment, whether for children, slaves, or husbands.

But though the sandal was common wear, there were also worn various sorts of slippers, shoes, half-shoes, and boots.

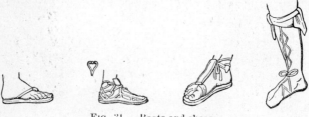

Fig. 31. — Boots and shoes.

The boots, which were supple and graceful, were worn in travelling, running, and hunting; while low shoes, black, white, or red, were often used in town, particularly when a guest was walking to a visit, and particularly to a dinner-party.

It may be observed in passing that shoes were the one article of dress in which Athenians allowed themselves something of our modern taste for novelty and numerous changes of fashion. If a dandy desired to be original he showed it in his shoes, not in his waistcoats. We hear of a number of shapes or styles called after the names of persons. Just as we speak of "Wellington" boots, and "Blucher" boots and "Gladstone" bags, so the Athenian spoke of "Alcibiades" shoes or "Iphicrates" shoes. But there is the difference, that with us the names are given by the manufacturers in questionable honour of the person named, while among the Athenians the name was given because the said person wore and set the

FIG. 32. — Men with sticks.

fashion of such articles. To wear nails in your shoes was commonly the mark of a rustic, although even a great dandy might affect such things in gold or silver. To wear mended or patched shoes was, according to Theophrastus, not good form for a gentleman.

If your shoes were not red or white, they were blacked with a gloss put on with a sponge. It is related of one citizen that "one of his friends met him, and when he saw his shoes well blacked, he was distressed to think he must be badly off, for he concluded that his shoes would never have been so well blacked if he had not blacked them himself."

Our typical citizen will certainly wear at least one seal-ring, partly for ornament and partly for use; he may even affect several rings, like Aristotle, who possessed the profoundest brain in Greece, but, nevertheless, had a pretty taste for self-adornment. But he must be careful not to make a parade of too many. They must not, as the comedian objects, come right down to his finger-nails. He will also usually carry a walking-stick. If an old man, his stick will usually have a curved or bent head, something like a shepherd's crook. These sticks were longer than ours and rather suggest those now used as wands of office. If a young blood, his stick will be straight, with a knob, and with a gold or silver ring or spiral round it. The professional and ostentatious philosopher will carry simply a stout club, to match his short cloak, long beard, and bare feet.

It has taken us a considerable time to get our Athenian citizen — whom we shall now call Pasicles for convenience of reference — fully dressed and out of doors. But by this time one can perhaps see him in his habit as he lived, with bare head, with tunic and mantle neatly draped, with sandals neatly bound on his feet, and a shapely stick in his hand.

He is followed, if possible, by two slaves, who are to be his carriers and errand-bearers, in case he wishes to buy anything, or to send a message home or to a friend. If he cannot afford two, he will at least have one, as practically indispensable to a gentleman. Should he be too poor even for one, he may hire a porter in the market-place for a special errand.

Thus followed, he will walk easily down towards the Agora, and, if he is a well-bred man, he will strike the happy mean between bustle and pomposity. The Athenians were very observant in such matters. They hated fuss and they hated arrogance. You must not "stalk," you must not hurry along, you must not be so little-minded as to be rolling your eyes all about the street. On the other hand, you must not look glum, with your eyes bent upon the ground. "Meidias," says Demosthenes, "stalks through the market-place with three or four attendants, talking cups and goblets, so that the passers-by can hear. . . . The town won't hold him." "To walk fast and talk loud" is conspicuously bad. According to Aristotle, the man of great self-respect has a "slow movement, deep voice, and composed speech."

As Pasicles is moving along, he perhaps passes a friend, who is riding out to visit his farm in the country, or to exercise a horse by jumping a few obstacles. Another he will meet walking to a visit. Another is going down to the Peiraeus. In such cases there is no bowing nor hand-shaking. To the Athenian, hand-shaking meant a good deal. It was either a solemn pledge, or, joined to a kiss like that of the Frenchman, a demonstrative welcome after long separation. To bowing the free citizen strongly objected; it was an act of obeisance and worship, and, as between mere mortals, it implied a superiority on one side which no Athenian would acknowledge. The orthodox greeting consisted of a bright look, and words which we may fairly translate as "Good day," or "Glad to see you," or "I hope you are well." A special social virtue lay in this easy courtesy.

Passing down between the various colonnades, among the

statues of gods and famous men, and under the plane-trees, Pasicles reaches the part of the Agora which is set apart for trade. Long ago, before dawn, the countryman has brought in his supplies, his cartload of wine or vegetables, and left them with the retail-dealers at their stalls, precisely as our market-gardeners come into our own markets. Poor women have brought in the yarn they have spun, or the flowers which they have worked into garlands. " My husband died," says one, " and left me with five little children, which I could hardly keep by plaiting garlands for the flower-market."

The various commodities for sale have long ago been set out in their special section of the market-place. The buyer knows exactly where to go to find bread or fish or green cheese or vegetables or oil, or to hire dancing-girls or a cook. Each kind of commodity has its own stand or " ring," and, if you wished to make an appointment in the market-place, you might tell your friend to meet you "at the fish" or "at the green-cheese" or "at the figs." Here were stalls or booths, almost precisely as you may see them any day in many modern markets. Round the market-place were shops, particularly of barbers, perfumers, shoemakers, saddlers, wine-sellers; and in the neighbourhood were the colonnades with their seats and grateful shade.

Though Athenian ladies who can afford to stay at home will never appear in the market, the purchasing being done by the husband or the slaves, yet poor Athenian women, mostly elderly, will be found there behind the stalls. As their special departments, they dealt chiefly in bread, figs, vegetables, and flowers. In the London market of Billingsgate it is the fish-women who have been notorious for abusive language; at

Athens it was the bread-women. "We need not," argues the comedian, "revile one another like bread-women." The mother of the poet Euripides is said to have sold vegetables. It is true that the average Athenian despised retail selling; nevertheless, to use contemptuous language towards man or woman for trading in the market was forbidden by law.

Our citizen will perhaps pass among the stalls in order to make some purchase, which he will send home by his slave. Around him will be heard, as in old London, the cries "buy vinegar," "buy oil," "buy charcoal," which the countryman in Aristophanes came to hate so much that he wished the word "buy" had never been known. But chiefly he will be attracted to the fish stalls. The Athenian was a modest eater and his weakness was not meat, but fish. Of all dealers the fish-mongers could afford to be the most independent, not to say insolent. One comedian calls them "assassins," another "burglars." Another describes their manner. You come along to bargain about fish — for of course at Athens you bargained and haggled over prices — and the fishmonger "pretends not to hear you, gives some big fish a slap, and, if he answers you, clips his words, and snaps out ''lev'npence.' If you ask him, 'How much for these two?' 'Half-crown!' 'That's heavy, will you take two shillings?' 'Yes, for one of 'em!' 'My good fellow, take two shillings and stop your jokes.' 'That's my price,' he answers, 'trot along with you.'"

To enable the buyer to get his fish fresh, a bell was rung when the new catch arrived at the market. And thereby hangs a tale, though not originally told of Athens itself. A musician was giving a recital on the harp to a gathering of his friends in a room near the market, when suddenly the fish-bell rang.

Up started all the company and left the room, except one rather deaf old man. The musician came to him and said, "Thank you, sir, for being the only man to have the manners to stay when the fish-bell rang." "What," said the solitary, "did you say it was the fish-bell? Thanks! Good-bye," and off he sped after the others.

The market, with all its manifold operations, is in full swing from about nine o'clock till towards noon. What we should call ten o'clock was called by the Athenians "full-market." About noon the stalls and wickerwork booths are cleared away and the ordinary business part of the day is done.

But during those business hours every sociable man in Athens will spend some time in or about the Agora. He must not, it is true, haunt the place, or he will be called an "agora-man," which practically means a loafer. Our typical citizen is of course sociable. Moreover he is to give a dinner-party to-night, and he must choose the fish, and hire a cook, and also girls to dance and play the flute. For ordinary purposes his own plain cooking at home will suffice, but for a special occasion he must engage one of those professional *chefs* who have been trained, or who profess to have been trained, at Syracuse in Sicily, where they understand good eating and drinking far better than they do at Athens. The situation is something like that when in modern times we engage caterers and special waiters. At Syracuse the dialect of Greek is Doric, and a *chef* will therefore ape the Doric in naming his dishes, very much as a modern *chef* will write a *menu* in which his concoctions bear names purporting to be French.

Then, perhaps, Pasicles will visit his banker. This

gentleman, who is very probably an Outlander, will be seated in a special portion of the square set apart for him and his *confrères*, and there, with a table in front of him, he will be engaged in cashing letters of credit from abroad, after he has tested the tokens, the signatures, and the marks of the signet-rings; or he will be changing foreign money for Attic money, or silver for copper, at a small commission; or he will be adjusting the ledgers as between two customers of his table. Meanwhile "the man of paltry ambitions" will be standing about this quarter, in order to make people fancy that he has large dealings with the banks. This method of banking might seem very crude and rather insecure; nevertheless we have no reason to believe that it was unsafe in any sense of the word. In speaking of money matters our Athenian will not ask "Who is your banker?" but "Whose table do you use?" and the expression is literally correct. A "banker" is a "table-man."

By this time — perhaps between ten and eleven — our friend Pasicles has finished his purchases and other business, and either takes a turn in the neighbouring colonnades, or else goes and sits in a shop, where he knows that he can meet his friends, and discuss either the news of the day, politics, or abstract questions mooted by persons philosophically inclined. Particularly affected for this purpose were the shops of the barbers, the chemists (or "perfumers"), and the doctors' waiting-rooms, although a shoemaker's was not a bad place, and on one occasion Socrates drops into a saddler's to provoke a little discussion. The shopkeeper had no objection whatever to thus turning his shop into a sort of clubroom; it was part of the business, and he enjoyed the talk as much as any one. So regular was this habit of dropping into a shop that in a speech of Demosthenes we find a complaint against a certain person as being "unsociable; he never visits any of the barbers' shops or perfumers' or the like." The barbers then, as until quite recently, were especially garrulous persons. "How will you have your hair cut?" said the barber to King Archelaus of Macedonia at the

FIG. 33. — Portraits: Herodotus and Thucydides.

time we are discussing. "In silence," replied Archelaus. Aristophanes observes somewhere that "there was much talk in the barbers' shops" to such and such an effect, and elsewhere he uses the phrase "when the fathers tell the boys in the barbers' shops."

The barber's business was to trim the hair and beard, to perform a complete manicure, and in general to make the customer presentable. He tucked a towel round you, snapped

his shears rhythmically, trimmed your hair, let you look at yourself in a bronze mirror, and then attended to your nails. Athenian taste was particularly exacting in the matter of the hair and hands. In the early part of our classical period it was usual to grow both the hair and the beard of medium length. Long ringlets like those of the English Cavaliers were affected only by boys and by the young bloods who formed the cavalry of Athens, and to wear long hair was so much a mark of rather assertive dandyism that the expression, "What are you long-haired for?" became practically equivalent to our expression, "What are you putting on airs for?" On the other hand, closely cropped hair was accounted more fit for a slave than for a free man. It generally marked the professional ath-

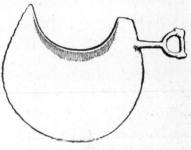

FIG. 34. — Razor.

lete, or the Stoic or Cynic philosopher, whose main concern was to flout fashion. What the Athenians considered the happy mean will at once appear from the illustrations opposite. A long and untrimmed beard was another mark of the professional philosopher.

Shaving was very rare in the early part of our period, but towards the end of it the Macedonian practice of shaving the face clean came into much vogue. But whatever else he might do, no Greek ever wore a moustache only. He might let his beard grow long, or he might trim it, or he might shave his face clean, but it would only be a barbarian — a Gaul for example — who would shave off the rest and keep the moustache.

The razor employed was shaped like a small sickle or half-moon, and one may doubt if the operation was very comfortable. The patient was apparently expected to assist. In a scene of Aristophanes the poet Euripides is made to say, "Agathon, you always carry a razor; lend me one." Replies Agathon, "Take it out of the case yourself." Whereupon Euripides proceeds "You're a gentleman. Now then (to his kinsman), sit down and puff out your right cheek."

Our citizen Pasicles may thus drop into various shops, but into one sort he must not be seen to go. These are the retail wine-shops, which correspond to the low public-houses of modern times. To sit in such a place, and there eat and drink, was not fit conduct even for a respectable slave. The thing was done nevertheless. Diogenes, it is reported, once caught sight of Demosthenes in such a place. Demosthenes was of course much alarmed, and tried to draw back out of sight, but Diogenes humorously cried, "You had better come out, Demosthenes; the more you draw back, the more you will be inside the shop.

Having nothing to say to such low haunts, Pasicles turns to go home for his luncheon. You may wonder how he knows what time it is, seeing that clocks and watches were not yet invented. Well, to begin with, the Athenians were not particular to a few minutes. There was none of the modern hurry and rush of life. There were no trains to catch, and in all engagements there was necessarily a certain amount of margin of punctuality. In the next place, they were far more accustomed than we are to watch the sun, and in a rough and ready manner to gauge his progress across the sky. In the

third place, for greater precision, they possessed for common
use a fairly practical form of public sundial.   This consisted of
a vertical staff, which threw a shadow upon a marked floor, and
the time was denominated by the length of the shadow, recorded
in feet.   Thus a guest was invited to come to dinner when the
shadow was "ten feet" or "twelve feet," as the case might be.
It is recorded of one hungry and greedy person that, when
invited for the hour of a twelve-foot shadow — which means the
evening shadow — he measured it in the early morning and
came soon after daybreak.   Another comedian improves upon
this and avers that he measured it by moonlight, and so came
in the night of the day before he was due.   There had been
invented also a really scientific sundial, but this was little used.
In the better houses there was often a sort of giant hour-glass,
through which, however, there ran water and not sand, and
the progress of the day was estimated by the quantity of water
which had run through.   In any case, we find no indication
that the Athenians were in any great degree inconvenienced by
their rough horological equipment.

As Pasicles is walking homewards, followed of course by
his attendant, he catches sight in the distance of an acquaintance whom he has not lately seen.   You will remember that
he is giving a dinner-party to-night.   He therefore orders the
slave to run on, overtake the friend, and say to him that
Pasicles invites him to dinner this evening when the shadow is
twelve feet.   There is nothing unusual in this short notice, nor
in the manner of delivering it.   Invitations were usually not
written notes ; they were regularly delivered either on a chance
meeting or else by a slave sent for the purpose.   There was no
formality or touchiness about Athenian social intercourse.

K

On arriving at his house our citizen will take his *déjeuner* —
a substantial, but not elaborate or protracted meal — generally

Fig. 35. — Man reading: tombstone.

under the covered portico or verandah of the courtyard, and in
the company of his family.   Then he will rest awhile through
the noonday heat, and perhaps read; but he will not, like the

Romans, take a siesta in the form of sleep. Sleep, indeed, plays a very small part in the catalogue of Athenian enjoyments or needs.

Feeling refreshed and vigorous, Pasicles sets out in the afternoon to walk to one of the three great public gymnasia in the suburbs of Athens — the Lyceum or Cynosarges or the Academy. Mostly he will find company on the way, inasmuch as there is a usual and understood hour for his friends to be making in the same direction.

The gymnasia were institutions extremely characteristic of Greek life in general, and especially of the life of Athens. Primarily they were intended for that bodily training upon which all Greeks set such immense store. With this training and its effects we have to deal later, when we speak of education. The gymnasia were entered only by men over eighteen, and those men must not be slaves. Persons of doubtful citizenship had access to that of Cynosarges alone. Here were grounds partly planted, but embracing open spaces for running, wrestling, boxing, spear-throwing, discus-throwing and leaping, the whole surrounded by terraces, colonnades, and rooms for punching the sack, dressing, anointing, and bathing, while statues of gods, heroes, victors, and famous men in general were dotted about. While the younger men are engaging with all vigour and emulation in these various sports, the older men may be taking the same exercise in milder forms, or indulging in various games of ball-play, somewhat as elderly men may be seen nowadays at tennis in the late afternoon. It must be premised, however, that the elderly Athenian was very careful not to render himself ridiculous or, as he expressed it, "cut a poor figure," by competing with the younger performers on their own ground.   It was not necessary that he should take any part at all.   From the terraces and colonnades round the enclosure he could look down at the sport and give his applause or make his comments, probably telling stories about the more excellent performers in the good old days, when he was young. Or, again, he might just as frequently ignore the entire proceedings, and devote himself to discussion, either of the news or of abstract and philosophic subjects, while he sat on the stone benches in the porticoes or walked up and down along the terraces.   Here you might see a citizen drawing a diagram in the sand with his stick and explaining to a company round him the geographical situation of some campaign or a problem in mensuration.   In another place a humorously ugly snub-nosed individual is the centre of a knot of persons arguing as to whether it is better to be a liar and not know it or to be a liar deliberately.   That is Socrates.   At a later date, in the Academy, a broad-shouldered but stooping citizen of highly intellectual and superior appearance may be developing rather transcendental doctrines in beautiful Greek to a circle of young and old admirers and non-admirers.   That is Plato.   In the Lyceum, at a still later day, on the terrace called "The Walk," an individual with a capacious skull and a distinct fancy for personal adornment may be working solidly down, in language not ornate, but effective, to the fundamental principles of politics, ethics, poetry, or logic.   That is Aristotle, the more human and interesting Herbert Spencer of ancient Athens.   All these are types of our chosen classical epoch, and they do not stand alone.   There are plenty of arguers and abundance of argumentation; there are jests and sarcasms; there is story-telling and the whole range of sociable conversation.

Games which are varieties of what we might call chess, draughts, or backgammon are indulged in by those who are so disposed. The whole place and its conduct are under the control of a special magistrate, who can eject disorderly persons and bad influences — including, it is gratifying to learn, the more truculent sophists.

In such surroundings Pasicles spends a couple of hours. He has perhaps sufficiently exercised both his mind and body, and is now disposed for his bath. Or he may postpone the bath for a while and take a walk in the avenue of the Agora. But the bath is indispensable, at least before a dinner-party. Many have seen the remains of the baths of Caracalla at Rome, or have read descriptions of the palatial establishments of that day, when every conceivable kind of hot, cold, vapour, and other bath was provided without stint. But one must not think of such establishments as existing in classical Athens. There we should find but a very modest equipment. Frequent bathing in hot water was regarded by the Athenians as effeminate, although neither the Romans nor the Japanese have found it so. There were, of course, hot baths, and even a sort of Turkish bath was not unknown, but for the most part the bath-houses were for cold bathing, and not very elaborate either. When we say "bath-houses" it is not implied that there were no baths in private houses. Every better house had something of the sort; but the bath-houses referred to were either provided by the state and entered on payment of a small fee, or were supplied by private enterprise. There were public baths at or near the gymnasia, but there must have been others in the city.

We should ourselves hardly consider the system of bathing

satisfactory.   There is mention, it is true, of a swimming-bath;
and there were certainly — as we see from pictures on the vases
— shower-baths, in the sense that you could stand under a
stream of water gushing from a spout.   But for the most part
you washed piecemeal from a large vessel, placed upon a stand,
the whole nearly resembling a baptismal font in a church.
Then the bathman and his assistants came round and poured
water over you from a bronze or earthenware vessel, which was
too shapely to be called a bucket, but which performed the

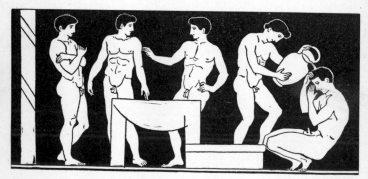

FIG. 36. — Youths bathing.

same duty.   Some persons did the pouring for themselves, but
this seems to have been in order to escape paying a small fee,
and was considered mean.   In the meantime it was just as well
to watch your clothes, for the baths were a favourite field for
the thieves who were known as " cloak-strippers."   And, by
the way, you must not sing in the bath.   Only boors did that.
A sort of soap, in the shape of fuller's earth, or of other
preparations from wood-ashes and special clay, might be
supplied by the bathman; but it was better to send your

slave along with your own perfumed supply, as well as with your oil-flask and your scraper. For these were necessary. After he has rubbed off the moisture, Pasicles will proceed to anoint himself with olive-oil mixed with perfume, and then he will take a curved and hollowed instrument of bronze, made for the purpose, and will scrape himself with great conscientiousness and care. Those who have seen the famous statue of the Apoxyomenos will at once understand the process.

After this our citizen dresses, perhaps chats awhile, and departs, much to the disappointment of a casual acquaintance, who has been hanging about the bath-house on the chance of getting an invitation to dinner at the last moment. Meanwhile the bathman, like the barber, is a great newsmonger and busybody, and knows and tells more about Pasicles than Pasicles ever knew about himself.

CHAPTER VII

CITIZEN'S SOCIAL DAY: DINNER, ETC.

PASICLES has again reached home, where he finds everything in readiness for the dinner. The slaves are neatly dressed and understand their business, the vessels are all well polished, and in a few minutes the guests will arrive.

Had this been a specially quiet day, our citizen would have dined with no one about him except his family and perhaps a chance friend. In that case he would himself have reclined on the couch, of which we shall speak immediately, while his wife would have been seated in a chair; the children would have come in for dessert and have disposed themselves on seats, or stood up, or clambered on the couch or on the mother's lap, according to their age and the manners and affection of the family. Of this family meal we have a rough illustration taken from a relief on a tomb. On the left is an attendant: on the right a descendant: the relief is connected with family worship.

To-day the wife will not appear, but will keep herself and the children in the women's quarters. The company will consist of men, and their conversation, if philosophic, would be above the women's comprehension, or, if not philosophic, it would cause the women no edification. The dinner is not to be a ceremony; it is to be a social enjoyment; and the full play of wit, wisdom, jest, anecdote, and appetite can be more harmlessly indulged when free from the restraint of female presence. And by this it is in no sense implied that there was necessarily anything which we need severely reprobate at a dinner-party of well-bred Athenian men.

The Athenians loved company at their meals, as at everything else. To eat your dinner alone was, according to Plutarch, "not dining, but feeding." Any special occasion

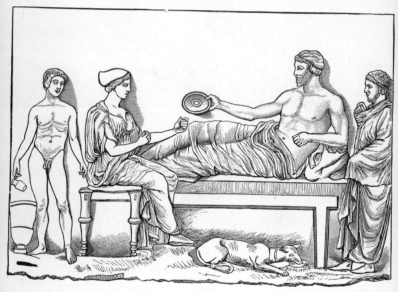

Fig. 37. — Family meal.

was an excuse for a banquet. It might be a birthday, the arrival or departure of a friend, the naming of a child, any important domestic event, or no event at all. And be it said, to their credit, that the actual consuming of food had comparatively little to do with the matter. There were doubtless some Athenians who liked good living for its own sake; there were doubtless even some gluttons; but the Athenians in general are not to be confused with the grosser feeders of Boeotia or the epicures of Corinth. One comedian remarks that an Attic dinner was very pretty to look at, but gave little satisfaction to the hungry interior. Both Plato and Xenophon wrote an essay in dialogue dealing with a dinner-party, and neither of them makes any mention of the food. A special abhorrence of the Athenian was " swinishness." The classical Attic ideal demanded enough well-served food to satisfy a reasonable appetite while pleasing the palate, but, first and foremost, lively society, conversation, and mutual entertainment. Different houses, different sorts of conversation; but always lively mutual entertainment.

As the guests arrive, the host simply greets them with a bright word and welcome look. In the large dining-room are placed the couches upon which the diners will recline at the meal. These are of some height from the ground, with frames of ornamental and inlaid woodwork and feet of ivory, or sometimes of silver; on them are coloured mattresses and cushions. The ordinary couch will accommodate two guests, or, in case of unexpected arrivals, three. And, speaking of unexpected arrivals, we must here remark that it was nothing exceptional for a guest who was an intimate friend of the house to bring along a companion, who had not received an invitation. This could not, of course, be done in modern times, when we sit on just so many chairs at a table of such and such a size. But in Athens there was no long table to sit at, more room could easily be extemporised, there was no individual supply of knives and forks, and the quantity of food, as has been said, counted for little in the affair. Accordingly, if A thought that

B, the uninvited, would be a welcome addition to the company, he brought B along with him. But be it remembered that the Athenians were gifted with all due social tact, and would use every discretion in such a practice. Sometimes, of course, the privilege was abused, and when a fashion grew up of the richer men attaching to themselves a sort of professional male companion — a "shadow" or "parasite" as he was called, when he was not called a toady — it became an expected thing that the shadow should accompany his chief to dinner, on the understanding that he might be more casually treated, and made the butt of much banter to which the invited guests would themselves object. But this fashion hardly belongs to our classical period.

In the *Banquet* of Plato we find this passage : " Aristodemus said that he met Socrates fresh from the bath and wearing low shoes, and, as the sight of the low shoes was unusual, he asked whither he was going so finely dressed. 'To a banquet at Agathon's,' he replied ; 'and I have put on finery because he is a fine man. What say you to going with me uninvited ?' 'Yes,' said Aristodemus, 'I will go with you, if you like.' On the way Socrates gets lost in a fit of abstraction, and Aristodemus actually goes in alone. He found the doors wide open, and was promptly led by a slave into the dining-room. Here the host met him and said: 'Welcome, Aristodemus; you are just in time to dine with us; if you have come on any other business, put that off and make one of us, as I was looking for you yesterday and meant to have asked you, if I could find you.'" We may suspect that this was a white social fib, but it at any rate illustrates the easy courtesy and hospitality of such occasions.

The guests having arrived, they first sit on the side of the couches, the slaves remove the sandals or slippers, and pour over their feet water, which was often scented, or else water and wine — for wine was very cheap. Then they proceed to recline on their left side, supported on their left elbow against the cushions. The position, therefore, is something between sitting and lying. If it is reasonably warm weather, the mantle is dropped from the shoulder to the waist, and the

FIG. 38.—Men reclining at banquet.

pictures show us that it was thus customary for men to dine extremely *décolletée*. It was meanwhile a point of good table manners to adopt the reclining position with case and grace. In Aristophanes the son is teaching the father how to be a man of the world. He says, "Come and lie down." "How?" asks the old man. "Gracefully." "Like this?" "Nothing of the sort." "How then?" "Stretch out your knees and shed yourself in an easy and supple way among the cushions. Then praise some article among the bronze-ware. Gaze at the patterns on the ceiling and admire the curtains of the court-yard." This therefore was etiquette, but it was only a toady who would keep taking up things and saying, "How beautiful this is!"

When all are in place, the servants come round with a vessel, from which they pour water over the hands of the guests. There are brought in small tables, light and orna-mental, one of which is set down before each couch for two persons, and on these are placed the several dishes as they come in order. The tables are lower than the couches, so that the right hand can reach down easily to them. Knives and forks there are none; the food is taken up in the fingers. It is true that, in dealing with very soft foods or gravies, or in extracting things from shells, spoons were not unknown, but usually the fingers were assisted simply by pieces of bread hollowed out for the purpose. It is clear that there was plenty of room for neatness and daintiness in handling food, and it was no small advantage to have fingers not too sensitive. This manner of eating will explain the remark in a comedian that if your "man who likes simple fare" can only get at certain luxuries, "may I be hanged if he will not swallow his very fingers." There were no napkins. Portions of soft bread, often specially prepared for the purpose, were used for wiping the fingers, and were afterwards thrown to the dogs, which might be present to catch them. But, apart from the dogs, it may be something of a shock to learn that the floor — which was, of course, with-out a carpet — was the receptacle for shells, bones, peelings, and other fragments, which were, however, swept out at a given stage of the proceedings. Conversation, meanwhile, must be general.

The first half of dinner consists of substantials, particularly fish and birds, eels, if they could be got, comparatively little meat (such as beef, lamb, and pork), and vegetables dressed to a degree of which we should hardly approve with oil, vinegar, honey, and sauces. During this part of the meal wine is not drunk. The Athenians kept their drinking as separate as possible from their eating.

Water is then brought round again, hands are washed, the tables are carried out, the floor is swept, a chant is sung to the accompaniment of the flutes, a libation of wine is poured out to the words "to the good genius," or "to good health," and the second part of the banquet begins. The tables are brought in again, and what we call dessert was for this reason called by the Athenians "the second tables." On these are placed fruits, fresh and dried, salted almonds, sweetmeats, cheese, and salt. "Attic salt," and to "eat a man's salt," are still proverbs among us derived from the Greeks.

The previous part of the banquet has been the dinner proper, and now begins what was known as the symposium, or the "drinking together." But it was by no means mere drinking; it was conversation, singing, jests, stories, listening to music, and watching dancing. On how high a level conversation might proceed, and theoretically should proceed, is shown to us by the dialogue-essays of Plato, Xenophon, and their imitator Plutarch, each entitled "Symposium" — the source whence we derive the meaning of the word as commonly used among ourselves.

The first thing to do was to pour a libation — which corresponds somewhat to our modern saying of grace — and then to elect a

L

"ruler" or "king" of the drinking. On him depended how much wine should be drunk, and of what strength it should be. And here let us say that, theoretically at least, moderation was a law of Attic life; and let us repeat that no tea or coffee was known, nor any other drinks except water and wine. Drunkenness was no more approved of among the Athenians than it is among ourselves. The only time at which it was right and proper was at the festivals of the god of the vintage. Otherwise it was probably just about as common as it was a generation or two ago. To drink neat wine was regarded as barbarous. The rather thick wines of Greece, such as the Chian and the Lesbian, were always mixed with water, either in the proportion of two of water to one of wine, or three of water to two of wine. Three to one was regarded as too weak, and a "drink for frogs." At a symposium one no more thought of drinking neat wine than we think of drinking neat whiskey. In the classical period they preferred rather sweet wine, whether red, white, or yellow, with a dash of some essence to give it a bouquet. In summer the wine was cooled by snow, which had been collected from the mountains, and was preserved by wrapping it in cloths and chaff. And this provokes an anecdote. The Greek word for dull, tedious, or monotonous is "cold" or "frigid." When Diphilus, the dramatic poet, was dining with a certain lady, he asked her how she managed to keep her wine so deliciously cold, and she sweetly replied, "I put one of your prologues into it." Age was, as now, a virtue in wine. Another witty lady, when presented with a small demijohn of wine, of which it was remarked that it was sixteen years old, replied, "It is very little for its age." That joke, we perceive, is somewhat old.

At our banquet the slaves proceed to mix, in a large and handsome vessel, the wine and water in due proportions; they then draw it out in equally handsome ladles or jugs, carry these to the guests, and fill their no less handsome cups or goblets.

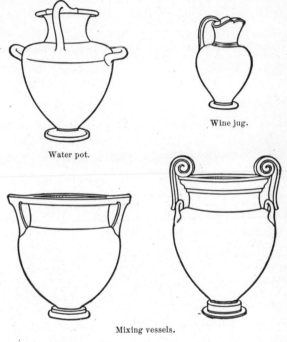

Water pot.

Wine jug.

Mixing vessels.

FIG. 39. — Vessels for feasts.

And here we may leave the drinking, with a repetition of the remark that a typical Athenian like Pasicles believed in moderation, in the amount which was cheering but not inebriating. Says one comedian, "The first cup means health, the second pleasure, the third is for sleep, and then wise man go home. The fourth means rudeness, the fifth shouting, the sixth disorder in the streets, the seventh black eyes, and the eighth a summons." Says Aristophanes, "Drinking is bad; for wine means banging at doors, hitting people and having to pay for it, and a headache into the bargain." And another, more to our purpose, observes, "This is the Greek way of drinking, to use moderate-sized cups, and chat, and talk pleasant nonsense to one another: the other course is swilling, not drinking, and it is deadly."

We need not pretend that there was not intoxication, and a great deal too much of it, but it mostly belonged to the younger

FIG. 40. — Drinking-cup.

men, and to a less orderly gathering than ours. There they drank healths and toasted ladies with a fine recklessness. Yet even the rakes hardly liked to say that a friend was "drunk." They said he was "wet," or "dipped," or "chest-protected."

Anything one may have read concerning expensive shows and elaborate entertainments after dinner has very little reference to this classical period. Generally flute-girls came in and played (Fig. 38); dancing-girls danced with much grace and expression; possibly a professional tumbler, man or woman, might perform such feats as dancing among swords; but often all these entertainments were discarded for conversation pure and simple. In the older days it was the fashion for a lyre to be passed along the company, each one who received it being expected to sing a catch of a certain type, and riddles were propounded to which ridiculous forfeits and prizes were attached; but these had become old-fashioned during our period. If you now sang at all, you were expected to sing something up-to-date, such as a lyric from the latest play of Euripides or some other dramatist.

After this the company separated. The slaves, who were in attendance, lighted their master through the streets with torches or else with oil-lamps enclosed in lanterns of horn; and Pasicles retired to bed, after seeing that the storeroom and the sideboard were properly sealed. . . . There were no after-dinner speeches.

Meanwhile what of the man who is poor? Might he resort to the gymnasia equally with the well-to-do? By all means, whenever he could find the time. He had as much right to walk there, sit there, and listen to what was said there, as any philosopher of them all. He could avail himself of the public baths, or sit and discourse in the shops along with the best of them. It is this fact, one may believe, which made him, as a democrat, trouble less about his mere pecuniary inequality than the modern radical in poverty is apt to trouble under the irritation of his complete social severance.

And seeing that the poor Athenian could not enjoy the luxuries of the dinner of a Pasicles, what did he live upon?

His staple articles of diet were barley porridge (with salt or honey), barley cake (something like the oat-cake of northern Britain), and barley loaves. To these he added vegetables, such as beans, peas, lentils, cabbages, and onions. Figs and olives were to be had for little. He was fond of thick pea-soup and lentil-soup, and he bought sausages and black-puddings. I am sorry to say that the sausage-dealers are accused by Aristophanes of making their wares occasionally of dog and donkey-meat; but that is a charge which never dies.   Meat and white wheaten bread a poor man seldom, if ever, tasted, but he obtained abundant supplies of salt fish, dried in slices and sent from the Black Sea in earthen jars. Also pilchards or sardines were plentiful and cheap. His drink was the wine of the country mixed with water, and such wine was purchasable at about a penny a quart.   On the whole, we may believe that the Athenian workingman enjoyed a diet which was at least as wholesome and plentiful as the diet of the ordinary English or Scottish labourer.

In one connection we have alluded to the young men of Athens and their amusements.   We shall not here deal with the details of fast life and wild oats.   The forms of these were in general those which are to be met with the world over.   They gambled with dice in dens and haunts intended for that purpose ; they trained race-horses and made bets upon them ; they armed the spurs of cocks, pheasants, and quails with a metal point, pitted them against each other on a board with a raised rim, and made bets upon the result.   And all these things, except perhaps the betting on race-horses, were theoretically disapproved by Athenian morals.   Nevertheless, cock-fighting held much the same position morally as prize-fighting once did in England.   It was disapproved in public, and considered no disgrace in private.   Alcibiades once went up to the Assembly, and there, becoming excited, forgot to keep his mantle closed, whereupon out flew a cock quail; but this betrayal of his propensities only caused laughter, and a sense that he was the same spirited fellow as ever.

Young men of the day, having no houses of their own in which to entertain their male friends, or not caring to take them there, indulged in various kinds of dinner-parties, at which there was anything but philosophic conversation, and a good deal of drinking. Such a dinner might be given by one of their number at some room lent or engaged for the purpose, or, very frequently, they formed themselves into a sort of club, providing the dinner by joint contribution. This might be done in two ways; the one was called "dinner by paying your shot" or "subscription dinner," the other "dinner by basket." The one expression explains itself; the "dinner by basket" means that each contributed, not money, but an actual portion of the supplies, which their respective slaves brought in baskets. This, of course, is the original sense of our word "picnic," and just as we are apt to hold picnics in the country or at the seaside, so the Athenian youth was given to sending the baskets to the shore and there compiling a feast, not so much for the love of external nature, as from a desire for freedom and novelty. Some of these coteries of youths gave themselves special names, not more respectable than those of the London young bloods of the early eighteenth century — the " Mohawks " and the " Tityrè Tus," and worse.

Like the young London rakes of Milton's day, they were apt, after a banquet, to issue into the streets "flown with insolence and wine." They then formed a procession, called a *Kômos*, headed by flute-players and accompanied by torches, and variously disported themselves. They serenaded ladies whom they knew; but chiefly they were notorious for forcing themselves into the houses of friends and acquaintances as a sort of after-dinner surprise-party, not always very welcome, but generally politely received. In the *Banquet* of Plato we read: "Aristophanes had begun to answer Socrates, when suddenly there was a great knocking at the door of the house, as of revellers, and the sound of a flute-girl was heard. Agathon told the attendants to go and see who were the intruders. 'If they are friends of ours,' he said, 'invite them in; but if not, say the symposium is over.' A little while afterwards they heard the voice of Alcibiades resounding in the court; he was in a great state of intoxication, and kept roaring and shouting 'Where is Agathon? Lead me to Agathon.' 'Hail, friends,' he said, appearing at the door crowned with a massive garland of ivy and flowers, his head flowing with ribbands; 'will you have a very drunken man as the companion of your revels? Or shall I crown Agathon and go away?'" In the sequel he does come in, and fair order prevails, while a philosophic discussion proceeds on love and literature.

And that is all we need find it necessary to say about the faster side of Athenian youth.

CHAPTER VIII

WOMAN'S LIFE AND FASHIONS

CHAPTER VIII

WOMAN'S LIFE AND FASHIONS

AT Athens, more than anywhere else in Greece, the woman was thrust, both publicly and socially, into the background. We must not confuse the Athenian woman of classical times with the free and influential Achaean woman of the days of Homer. We have already given some explanation of the difference, but we may repeat here that it was partly due to the peculiar racial character of the Athenians, more to the altered conditions of life in a populous and closely packed city, and still more to the extremely democratic life of the male Athenian, which made his home of comparatively little account.

It has already been remarked that, when women had thus become secluded, their sphere of operations limited, their character weakened, and their education neglected, it became customary to look upon them as naturally and inevitably inferior to men, both intellectually and morally. This was not only the opinion of the vulgar, it was held by philosophers like Aristotle. Experience and observation of women, as they were, led him to take for granted that woman was "in general an inferior being," and it was only an unusually and audaciously speculative Plato who could suggest that the difference was due rather to circumstances than to nature. Yet even in Plato the special excellence of a woman is elsewhere stated to be "to

155

keep house well and obey her husband." It would be easy to collect numerous utterances of poets, philosophers, and orators, to support this text, and also that of Ajax in Sophocles, "Woman, women are adorned by silence."

The Athenian did not, it is true, keep his wife imprisoned after the manner of the Turk, nor did he entertain so low a view of her relation to himself; but he did theoretically maintain that, unless on special occasions and for good and sufficient cause shown, her place was inside the house, and her range limited by the street door. In practice she enjoyed much more liberty, but this was at least the theory.

It follows that, since her functions were so limited, her education as a girl was correspondingly meagre. If she learned to read and write, or play on a musical instrument — as she certainly often did — it was not according to a recognised system of education. The mother or some attendant might impart this knowledge, if she possessed it; but the usual feeling of the Athenian was one expressed in Euripides, that a woman was none the better for being too clever intellectually. Her youthful training was therefore directed towards her domestic duties. She learned spinning and weaving and working embroidery, so that she might do these things in her own household, and also teach and direct her female slaves in these arts. She also learned plain cooking and domestic management; for she would eventually be called upon to conduct a household of both male and female servants and to control the storeroom. But beyond this her education did not go. "To see as little as possible, to hear as little as possible, and to ask as few questions as possible," is Xenophon's statement of the ideal educational career of a girl.

As a little child her life was probably happy enough. She had the domestic courtyard to play in, and she was furnished with toys and pet animals to play with. Dolls of earthenware or wax, painted and furnished with movable legs and arms, were abundant. Swings were hung under the verandah in the

Fig. 41. — Swing.

court. Mothers and nurses were kind, and she might be taken up to the roof of the house to see processions in the streets. Her little brothers played about with her till their seventh year. She might come in to dessert when dinner was but a family affair, and her mid-day meal she often took with her parents in the court.

As she grows older she receives the domestic instruction before mentioned, and the nearer she comes to marriageable age the more regard she must have to modesty of deportment. Theoretically the unmarried girl must not be seen outside the middle door, which separates the women's quarters from those of the more open house. If she goes abroad, it is with some elder female in charge, in order to take part in one of the great festive religious processions, or in a funeral ceremony, or to visit some temple. So far as she is seen of men, it must be on such occasions, and, so far as she herself sees other men than those of her immediate family, it must be either then or when she peeps from the window in the upper storey, or is permitted to look down from the roof into the street on procession days. There was thus little opportunity among the well-to-do classes for falling in love, whether at first sight or at any time. Nevertheless such a thing did very occasionally happen, and Athenian youths, it may be remarked, were highly inflammable. To them beauty made strong appeals, and the appeal was not weakened by the sense of difficulty and mystery.

Yet, after all, love mattered little so far as the girl's future was concerned. Let us imagine her to be now of marriageable age, which may be anywhere from fifteen to twenty. We will, for convenience, call her Pasiclea. Pasiclea's father or other guardian—if not her father, her nearest male kinsman — is prepared to give her a dowry of certain dimensions, and he is looking about for a suitable match. If she has no father, the nearest male kinsman, provided he is a bachelor himself and is not a full brother nor in the direct line of descent, has the first claim to marry her himself. If he is unable or disinclined, he either fixes his eyes upon some suitable citizen, perhaps quite young, but preferably upwards of thirty or thirty-five, or he employs for the purpose a professional matchmaker — a woman, one need hardly say. It is, of course, the most natural proceeding to consider first the circle of his acquaintance and the sons of his friends, but, before all things, equality of pecuniary position is sought on both sides. The Athenians had in this connection the proverb "keep to your own track." If Pasiclea's father or guardian knew of no suitable match, the matchmaker discovered one for him, although, truth to tell, it was probably more commonly her task to find and win over a suitable wife for some man whose time had come to settle down.

Meanwhile the proposed bridegroom was being induced to marry by one of two considerations. For the most part marriage was felt to be a burden and an embarrassment. According to Euripides, woman was a "necessary evil." We must, it is true, discount the attitude of Euripides. When it was remarked to Sophocles that his brother poet was a woman-hater, he replied "Yes, in his tragedies." Nevertheless, the attitude of the poet was fairly general. The legislator Solon was asked to penalise bachelors, but he could not find it in his heart, for, he said, " a wife is a heavy load to carry." If therefore an Athenian who had enjoyed no opportunity of falling in love was considering matrimony, it was either because his father was insisting upon it, or because of a consideration which is nowadays not quite so easy to understand, but which was then exceedingly potent. Every citizen desired to leave behind him some one, not merely for the usual and natural motives, such as to continue his family and inherit his possessions, but, before and above all, to bury him and pay due honours to his body and his tomb. The attitude of the Athenian towards the after-world belongs to the discussion of Athenian religion, but thus much should be said here, that the comfort and honour of the dead in the region beyond death were held to depend upon the attentions paid to the corpse and to the place where it was buried. A ghost who had no posterity on earth was in a lamentable plight in Hades. Apart from the pressure of public opinion and ideas of good form, from the encouragement of the state, and from considerations of his old age and its environment, the citizen had this strong motive prompting him to undertake what otherwise he might have been disposed to avoid.

Well, a match for Pasiclea is made. If it is ideal, she will be about eighteen, and her future husband about thirty-two. Women aged rapidly in Greece, and this difference of age was therefore regarded as some sort of adjustment.

The first and most important ceremony was the betrothal, at which, by the way, it was not in the least necessary that the girl should be present. Properly speaking, the affair is a contract between persons entitled so to contract, and the girl has no standing in the matter. A dowry is agreed upon, and a solemn "pledging" is performed in the presence of witnesses. Without this "giving away," as it was called, an Athenian marriage is invalid. There was no such thing as a marriage in the presence of priests or of representatives of the state. Indeed there was no church at all in our sense of the word. The only ceremony after the pledging was the "fetching home," which took place at a later day and which we may regard as the actual wedding. This previous solemnity before witnesses was therefore indispensable. So far as the dowry was concerned, it belonged to the wife, must be given back if she was divorced, and when she died, it went, not to her husband, but to her nearest of kin. A consequence of this position was that a wealthy wife sometimes became the predominant partner and kept her husband in submission to the power of the purse.

The actual wedding of Pasiclea will take place when the moon is near the full, and probably in the winter. Before the ceremony sacrifices to the gods of marriage will be made in both houses, and a sort of sacramental bathing will be *de rigueur*. The groom, perfumed and dressed in his gayest, and wearing a wreath, arrives, together with his best man, his parents, and his friends at the home of the bride, which he finds decorated at the doors with olive and laurel boughs. There the marriage feast is prepared, and prominent at that feast is the good old wedding-cake, made, at Athens, chiefly of pounded sesame-seeds mixed with honey. On this occasion the men and women for once feast together, but the women do not recline; they are seated together on the opposite side of the room from the men. The bride is all the time veiled, and some of the party, even including the groom, may never have seen her face. Nevertheless, the party is festive and conversation is general, as we perceive from a passage in Theophrastus, who, talking of the *gaucheries* committed by the Inopportune Man, remarks that " when he is a guest at a wedding he is the sort of man to run down the female sex." The feast over, and evening having come, a flute-player is heard at the door; the respective mothers light each a pair of torches; the bride, veiled all the time, is led out to a carriage or some sort of vehicle, where she seats herself between the groom and the best man, who are standing. Before them go the flute-players, and before and around them a procession of friends, singing that hymeneal

M

song which, in its inevitableness, corresponds somewhat to our wedding march. Behind walks the mother of the bride, carrying her torches. Meanwhile the people in the streets cheer them and wish them joy with no little blending of facetiousness. At the bridegroom's door, which is also decorated, the bride is formally received by his mother; confetti are scattered over the party; Pasiclea eats a piece of quince — an emblem, possibly, because of its bitter-sweetness, of our

FIG. 42. — Marriage procession to fetch the bride.

"for better or worse" — and she is led into the house. A chorus of girls sing a song known as the epithalamion, and the party disperses.

On the following day, which is called the "unveiling," the newly married couple are "at home" to their friends. Sometimes they have already been honoured by a morning song at the door. Pasiclea unveils herself, and receives the wedding presents which the visitors have brought, including vases, dishes, slippers and sandals, mirrors, combs, soaps, perfumes, and whatsoever other things were most affected before fish-slices and hair-brushes were invented.

From this time forward she is mistress of the house, allots duties, and dispenses stores. She wakes the slaves, if necessary, in the morning, instructs them in their tasks, and carries the keys. She will herself perform a fair amount of spinning and

Fig. 43. — Girl with distaff.

weaving. At the latter she will get no little exercise, and, if she does her work in the courtyard, a fair amount of fresh air also. She must be strict in her discipline, for the Athenian slave had his or her foibles. There were, it is true, no cats, but weasels and harmless snakes were employed to keep down the mice, and when anything was broken, or when food mysteriously disappeared, it was usual for the slave to declare that "it must have been the weasel." Pasiclea is herself a young lady of proper instincts. She is not wasteful, and she does not drink wine, as some older and less refined Athenian women appear to have done too frequently. Her husband will, therefore, never be guilty, as others sometimes were, of the severity, or the meanness, of locking up the storeroom and sealing the door.

Her position is beyond question entirely subordinate, but it is one in which she is respected and can respect herself. Her

Fig. 44. — Penelope at her loom.

husband may, or may not, permit her to talk politics at lunch or family dinner. That wives often did this, or attempted it, is certain. Complains one lady in Aristophanes: "Then we would ask: 'Husband, how came you men to bungle this business so stupidly?' And he would promptly scowl and say that if I didn't attend to my spinning, I should be very sorry for myself." Yet even if her spouse were thus contemptuous, there were two things which, if he was a gentleman, he would not do. He would not permit any man to speak rudely or unbecomingly in the presence of his women-folk, and he would not put himself in any undignified position which would humiliate him before them. Demosthenes, in a famous passage, enlarges on the mortification of a man who is compelled to hide from an unreasonable arrest by climbing over his neighbour's roof, or creeping under a bed, or otherwise cutting a poor figure "in the sight of his own wife, to whom he betrothed himself in the character of a free man and a citizen of the state." Nor is there any reason to disbelieve that the domestic relations were often accompanied by a tolerable degree of affection on either side.

Yet, with all this, Pasiclea's married life would be regarded in these days as extremely monotonous. During her younger years, at least, she will be kept much within doors. If she goes out, it will be theoretically with her husband's consent, and accompanied by a female attendant. Even if the husband was indulgent, public opinion had to be consulted. According to one of the orators, "the woman who goes out of doors ought to be of such an age that those who meet her may ask, not whose wife she is, but whose mother she is."

We may, perhaps, be of opinion that all this insistence of good advice on the part of poets and orators is but a sign that the strict rule of seclusion was a good deal honoured in the breach. We know that women often did walk out with their attendants, that they certainly went out occasionally to purchase things, that they paid visits to each other and talked gossip and dress, and that they sometimes asked each other to lunch. Moreover, there were certain recognised occasions on which they were expected to move abroad. They went to the theatre to see the tragedies performed, although apparently they were not allowed, or at least countenanced — and a good thing too — at the comedies. They went to the great processions, and to the mysteries. There were certain religious festivals which belonged exclusively to women. They went also, as we have seen, to weddings, as well as to funerals and to various festivities and ceremonies connected therewith.

In the house itself they had their work, often their music, their children, and it must not be forgotten, a number of female slaves, who were mentally quite as cultivated as themselves. What Pasiclea might be like when at home we can discern from illustrations such as those here reproduced. The

Fig. 45. — Women at home.

lady seated on the left is working on a frame, the lady on the right is using unguents.

Only too frequently the women — though not, of course, our good Pasiclea — were given to peeping out of the door or the upstairs window into the street. Says a chorus of women in Aristophanes: "You were always calling us the very mischief. If we are the mischief, why do you marry us? And why do you forbid us to leave the house or to be caught peeping out? And if the wifey goes out anywhere, and you find her not at home, you get mad as mad can be. And if we take a peep out of window, you try to get a look at the mischief. And if she is abashed and draws back, you are all the more eager to see the mischief taking another peep!"

Nor let it be forgotten that, though legally and by custom subordinate, the woman had ways of her own of reversing the position. There were plenty of men who from uxoriousness or weakness of character, or because they had married money or a vixen, were "ruled by the slipper." Perhaps it was in joke that Themistocles declared that his child ruled Greece: "For Athens rules Greece, and I rule Athens, and my wife rules me, and the child rules her." On the other hand, the scolding Xanthippe, the wife of Socrates, was by no means a joke. A speech of a plain old squireen in Aristophanes is worth reciting: "I wish to goodness the matchmaker had come to a miserable end, who induced me to marry your mother. For I thoroughly enjoyed my rustic life, untidy in the rough, free-and-easy, all among the bees and sheep and olive-cakes. But then I married the niece of Megacles the son of Megacles — a countryman like me, marrying a city madam, a haughty pampered Lady Vere de Vere! . . . And afterwards, when this son was born to me and this good wife of mine, then we began to wrangle and abuse one another about his name. She wanted to tack *hippos* to it — Xanthippos or Chairhippos or Callippides, — while I was for giving him my grandfather's name, Pheidonides. So for awhile we quarrelled, but at last came to an agreement and called him Pheidippides" — which is very much as if she wanted to call him Marmaduke, while he preferred Hodge, and they compromised with Hodgaduke.

In a previous chapter we contrived so to dress our Athenian

male citizen that his appearance became, we may hope, tolerably clear. One may shrink from attempting the same task with Pasiclea. After studying all the obtainable descriptions and examining all the obtainable pictures and diagrams, we may have learned to know very well how the various dresses and arrangements of dresses look and ought to look, but in several of the more complicated instances we may still be somewhat confused as to exactly how they were put on.

FIG. 46. — Putting on the tunic.

It is perhaps best, therefore, to content ourselves with giving a general description and offering such illustrations as seem most helpful. A member of the sex concerned will perhaps see at a glance how the thing was done, while the male reader will probably care only for the result.

As with the men, the female attire consisted ordinarily of two chief portions, the light under-dress and the heavier mantle or shawl, both of them properly bearing the same Greek names as those of the men. With the women, however, there was naturally more variety of shape or make, and various other names, not too precisely understood, are applied in virtue of difference of details. What in the case of the man is the tunic, is in the case of the women both longer and fuller. The girdle also was wider and more important. The tunic may be sleeved or sleeveless, and its sleeves may be close or bell-shaped. It is commonly fastened with a brooch or pin over the right shoulder and mostly has a double fold over the breast. Decorated with a border, and itself most frequently of saffron colour, it served as the ordinary attire for the house; and very graceful it can look, as some at least

FIG. 47.— Women's tunics.

of the figures in the illustrations may show. Unlike the tunic of the men, it often trailed behind.

For out-of-doors and visiting the upper garment was put on and carefully draped round the body, sometimes even being drawn over the head, if a separate headcover or veil was not employed. For be it remembered that the women, like the men, wore no hat, except in the country, when a large sun-hat was allowed. This upper garment also was more diversified than that of the other sex.

In respect of material we find not only woollen, cotton, and ordinary linen, but also a fine kind of material of which the exact nature is not known, but which could apparently be made diaphanous and suggests muslin. Towards the end of our period manufactured silk is finding its way into Athenian households. In respect of colours, we find in particular saffron, purple, apple-green, olive-green, grey-blue, golden-brown, and white.

FIG. 48. — Doric girl's dress.

And here, in order to show that in matter of dress and its interest the eternal feminine was the same in ancient Greece as in modern Everywhere, we may cull a passage, from a poetical genre-sketch by Theocritus. In view of what we have learned concerning the restrictions upon Athenian women, it must indeed be premised that the scene is at Alexandria, where women doubt-less enjoyed more freedom than at Athens, and also that it was written there some two generations later than our period. Nevertheless, in general, it would serve for a fairly vivid picture of Athenian *bourgeois* life on a day of festival. Gorgo calls upon Praxinoe on the feast of Adonis. An infant, Zopyrion, and Eunoe, the maid, are present. The conversation proceeds thus: —

Gor. Is Praxinoe in?

Prax. My dear Gorgo! At last! Yes, in. It's a wonder you come at all. Look for a chair for her, Eunoe. And put a cushion in it.

Gor. Thanks; don't trouble.

Prax. Sit down.

Gor. The foolishness of me! I have hardly got to you alive, for the crowd and the four-in-hands. Boots and swaggering soldiers everywhere! And the journey is interminable! My dear woman, you live quite too far afield.

Prax. Yes, that insane creature came to the ends of the earth and bought a hole, not a house to live in, just to stop us from being neighbours; out of spite, the jealous wretch — always his way.

Gor. Don't speak of your husband like that, my dear, before the little one. My good woman, see how he is looking at you! Never mind, Zopyrion, sweet child; she doesn't mean daddy!

Prax. The bairn is taking notice, I declare.

Gor. Nice daddy!

Prax. Yes, and the other day that daddy was to buy soda and rouge from the market, and came back with salt — for all he's a man twenty feet high!

Gor. My man Diocleides is just the same — throws money away! Yesterday he bought five fleeces — seven shillings for dog's hair, pickings from old bags, nothing but dirt, endless work! But come, get your gown and shawl.

Prax. Eunoe . . . move yourself! Be quick with some water! . . . You silly thing! why are you wetting my dress? That will do! Please heaven, I have had some sort of a wash. Where is the key of the big chest? Bring it here.

Gor. Praxinoe, that full gown is very becoming. Tell me, how much did it come to, before it was off the loom?

Prax. Don't mention it, Gorgo. More than eight guineas, good money down! And then I worked myself to death over it.

Gor. Well, it has turned out a success.

Prax. It is kind of you to say so . . .

Bring me my shawl, and put my sun-hat on properly . . .

I shan't take you, child. Bogey-man! Horse bites! Cry as much as you like; we must not have you crippled. Let us be going. Phrygia, take the little one and play. Call the dog inside. Shut the front door.

The hair of the Grecian women was generally long and rich, and infinite pains were spent on dressing it with taste and elegance. According to the Athenian ideal it should be wavy, display not too much forehead, and should be either blue-black or golden. Golden, being the rarer colour, was one much affected by those ladies who systematically improved upon nature. The fashion of dressing the hair was subject to much variation, but even at one and the same date the Athenian woman sought no monotonous uniformity. They were satisfied if the result was graceful and becoming. When

FIG. 49.—Women's hair (ideal); from coins.

the hair had been drawn in graceful curves into a knot or ball at the back of the head, it was sometimes kept in place by a net of threadwork — gold thread by preference; sometimes a strip or band of coloured material was wound artistically round it; on less showy occasions it is to be seen depicted as enclosed in a complete bag or bladder. Combs and pins were also used, and, in fullest dress, a golden or gilded coronal or frontlet stood up in the same place on which ladies now wear a tiara. Perhaps a far clearer notion will be formed at once from a glance at a few illustrations than could be derived from any amount of description.

The footwear of women consisted of sandals, of white

slippers which would fit either foot, of easy yellow shoes, and occasionally of soft high boots. Fans of peacocks' feathers or simply of light wood, and a parasol for out-of-doors, are other articles of equipment.

For ornaments, both of girls and matrons, there were worn gold earrings (spirals or with drops), gold necklets, gold bracelets on the upper arm (mostly shaped like snakes), rings, and frequently gold bands on the ankles. The mother of

Fig. 50. — Woman with fan.

Alcibiades, we are told, wore " perhaps £500 worth," if we may venture once more to modernise the value of money.

And here, perhaps, we ought in chivalry to stop. But our duty is to be historical first and chivalrous afterwards, and we are therefore bound to add that many Athenian women adopted every known device for improving Nature's handiwork. When they were too short, they of course wore high cork soles to their shoes. The Athenians did not believe in wasp-like waists, but, if their figure was distinctly not perfection, they did not shrink from padding or from physical compression. They not only anointed their hair — as every one was supposed to do — but they dyed it, and wore false additions. They were liberal with rouge, vegetable dyes, white-lead, and other prep-

FIG. 51. — Greek mirror.

arations. They rubbed lampblack or sulphuret of antimony under their eyes and on the eyebrows. Xenophon has a rather Sandford-and-Merton little treatise on model housekeeping, and in this the somewhat pedantic and priggish husband warns his wife that perspiration or tears will betray her, and he asks what she would think of *him* if *he* came in be-rouged. As if, forsooth, she was chiefly considering him! More effective is the comic poet, who thus remonstrates with one lady when she overdoes the thing: "If you go out in summer, from your eyes there run two streaks of black; from your cheeks perspiration makes a red furrow down to your neck; and when your hair touches your face it gets white with white-lead." Beyond this, perhaps, we must not pry. Moreover, our good Pasiclea has little to do with such things.

CHAPTER IX

BOYHOOD — EDUCATION AND TRAINING

BOYHOOD — EDUCATION AND TRAINING

TIME has passed and Pasiclea has a son. The outer door is decorated with an olive branch in honour of that event. By that sign it is known to all whom it may concern that the child is a boy. Had it been a girl, a fillet of wool would have been seen instead. The father is much rejoiced, for girls were regarded with less favour, and, in poor houses, as rather a burden. So far did this prejudice go that Athenian mothers were sometimes known to substitute some other woman's male child for their own female offspring. Occasionally the child was not merely an exchange, but entirely supposititious. Demosthenes, speaking of a virulent opponent, says: " His real mother was the most sensible of women ; she sold him as soon as he was born. His supposititious mother was the most foolish, for she bought him when she could have bought a better for the same money."

And here we must say a word concerning a most distressing feature in ancient Greek life. It was optional for a father to rear his child or not. To put it crudely, he had the absolute disposal of it; if he were very poor, or if the child were deformed, or if he chose to entertain any other motive for the act, he could expose the infant to live or die. The practice, of course, dates from a time when food was scarce and life was a terrible struggle. We must not suppose that such exposure was very frequent on the part of true Athenian citizens of our period. — There was necessarily a reasonable amount of natural affection; there was the maternal influence; there was the drag of public opinion; there was the desire of possessing children to honour one's own sepulchre. Nevertheless, the practice was one fully recognised as legal, and the poor availed themselves of it, particularly in the case of unwelcome female children. The usual proceeding in such cases was to place the infant in a large earthenware vessel or pot, and leave it, either in the precincts of a temple or in some other place where it would easily be found. It is tolerably certain that the child was very seldom left to perish. Vulgarly they called this "potting" the child. If any person who found it chose to bring it up, he could reckon it as his slave, or employ it as he would; and mothers were therefore in the habit of attaching to the exposed infant certain tokens, in the shape of trinkets or amulets, by which a possible recognition might take place in the vague future.

Pasiclea's little boy, however, runs no such risk. He is only too welcome. After he had been bathed in water and

oil, he is wrapped in swaddling-clothes, after a fashion which makes him look something between a chrysalis and an Indian papoose. A long strip of cloth is

Fig. 52. — Cradle.

wound round and round him. He will subsequently occupy a cradle, generally shaped like a shoe, which is either hung up and swung to and fro, or else rocked with the feet.

A few days after the birth — on the fifth, seventh, or tenth day — there takes place a little ceremony, in which the child is carried by the nurse at a run round a fire blazing on the family hearth, and at which he is acknowledged by the father. On the tenth day, whether the aforesaid ceremony occur on that day or have preceded it, there is a festive gathering, a special cake is eaten, and the child receives his name. The proceedings remind one forcibly of a christening, both in this respect and also because of the presents made to the child. Among these are commonly included little charms or amulets to be worn as means of averting the evil eye. The boy receives but one name, and at Athens, it may be remarked, some names were of a more aristocratic colour than others. As old family names they suggested what the Americans call "first families." It was a much finer thing to be called Megacles than Pheidon. But there was nothing to prevent the meanest Athenian from calling his son by the equivalent of Plantagenet or De Montmorency. The favourite name for the eldest son was that of his paternal grandfather, so that a pedigree was apt to run thus: Aristides, Lysimachus, Aristides, Lysimachus, — and so on *ad infinitum*. This was, however, in no way binding, and if Nausinicus so chose, he could call his son Nausinicus also, or change half the name and call him Nausiphilus, or, in short, do exactly as he pleased. There was also nothing, except the practical inconvenience, to prevent a man in after life from changing his name, either to a more aristocratic appearance, as from Simon to Simonides, or from Tromes to Atrometus, or else adopting a nickname, as in the case of Plato, whose true name was Aristocles, but who was called "Plato" from his broad shoulders.

Well, let us call Pasiclea's little boy Lysimachus, and take him through the pilgrimage of his childhood. It is highly probable that he will be nursed by a foster-mother, who will rock his cradle, sing him lullabies and charms to keep off the evil eye, and teach him to walk.   Or an elderly slave woman will take him in charge, chastise him with the slipper when he is naughty, and frighten him with wolves and bogeys who take numerous shapes and perhaps eat people.   She will teach him nursery rhymes, and will tell him all manner of legends of a mythological character, and also fables of Aesop.   Her regular mode of beginning is " Once on a time there was . . . ," or " So there was once . . . . "   Her stories will not always contribute to his intellectual development, and both Plato and Aristotle look with disfavour upon the mental effects of the " old wives' tales " as impressed in early childhood.   But the fables of Aesop were deemed good, and not to know your Aesop is equivalent to having had no decent education.

Till his seventh year the little Lysimachus is reared in the women's quarters.   He has plenty of playthings ; rattles, balls, hoops, whip-toys and spinning-tops, toy carts and the like. His father is good to him, and the rustic old gentleman, whom we have already had occasion to quote from Aristophanes, describes how, with the first obol he ever got for serving on a jury, he bought his little boy a little waggon.   He has also pet animals, little dogs, tortoises, ducks and other birds.   The little fellow at this period of his life has been already depicted in an illustration.   The impulse to plastic art was so strong by instinct and example at Athens, that the child himself is always modelling and making things out of clay or wax or fruit-peel.

But, says Plato, the boy is " the most unmanageable of animals," and therefore in his eighth year his lot begins to be somewhat less pleasant.   He is taken from the women's domain and handed over to a male slave, known as the *paedagogus* (see Fig. 54), who is to look after his goings and comings, take him to and from school, and generally superintend his manners. This worthy, with his beard and cloak and long stick, is a familiar figure in drama and in the paintings on vases. He is not a teacher or schoolmaster, and our use of the word "pedagogue" differs widely from the Greek sense. He is rather a bear-leader. In theory he should be an elderly person of superior character and some cultivation. In practice he was often simply a slave who was past active work or otherwise unfit for it.

When the boy goes to school or elsewhere the paedagogus will walk behind him, carrying his books, writing-tablets, and musical instruments, and seeing that he speaks to no one, carries himself properly, and fixes his eyes modestly on the ground. At home he will watch his manners and habits, seeing that he uses his left hand for the bread but his right hand for other food, and that he keeps silence in the presence of his elders and gets up from his seat when they enter. He will not permit Lysimachus to sit cross-legged nor with his chin propped on his hand. To prevent these things he may scold or use his stick. The well-bred Athenian attached the greatest importance to such details of life. According to Plato they "were more careful for good manners and behaviour than for reading and writing and playing music." There were, of course, weak and inefficient slaves in this position, and all along it must be understood that only the better classes could afford all this careful provision for their boys. In point of fact, boys played a good deal in the streets, whipping their tops, playing at duckstone, tug-of-war, games of catching, blind-man's-buff, "odd or even," and "how many fingers do I hold up?" They tied cockchafers by the leg and let them fly. They had a game corresponding to marbles, but played with nuts, which they pitched into a hole.

But our young friend Lysimachus is receiving an ideal education, and to school he goes with his paedagogus behind him. It is not a boarding-school, nor a public school, for there are no such things; but it may be a school of no small size, with perhaps a hundred pupils or more. The numbers necessarily varied according to the repute of the master. At one music school — and music was an essential part of education — the master had only two pupils. But he naturally had statues of the appropriate gods, to wit, the nine Muses and also Apollo, the god of music. When asked how many persons were at his school, he therefore replied, "By the help of the gods, twelve."

Education at Athens was not undertaken by the state, nor was it absolutely compulsory from a legal point of view. The state expected, and public opinion insisted, that all male citizens should be educated, but the only legal measure bearing upon the matter was the provision that a son to whom an education had not been given was not bound — as others were — to support his father in old age. And here one cannot refrain from drawing attention to the something superior in the Greek mind which caused the Greeks to set a value on education, and to direct it with an intelligence unknown to any ancient people before them. In this they were altogether original, and modern Europe owes them more than we can now estimate.

Their scheme embraced reading and writing, literary appreciation, music both vocal and instrumental, physical training, and, somewhat later, towards the end of our period, arithmetic and drawing. Swimming was also regularly taught. They had no thought of education serving as a means to technical skill or a livelihood ; they thought of it as a means to self-culture and worthy citizenship. To train the intellect, the passions, and the body, was the aim of Athenian culture. It is on this course that Lysimachus now enters.

He will begin with the teacher of A B C; and there in his class he will learn his letters and chant his *b-a ba, b-e be*, and the rest, until he can read. His master will then teach him to write, tracing the letters faintly for him to go over and deepen, and guiding his hand. This will first be done on those waxed tablets with a raised rim which answer to our slate, until the pupil is proficient enough to be trusted with the more expensive papyrus-paper and the split reed which serves as a pen. On the tablet he scratches in the stiffened wax with a pointed style or metal instrument, very much as if one wrote on thickly buttered bread with a small stiletto (Fig. 53).

He will not, we gather, be encouraged either to love or to respect this elementary teacher. The stick and the strap were much in evidence, and, in any case, to teach A B C was regarded as the most miserable of occupations. It was often the last resort of persons who could do nothing else. A proverb went concerning the man who had "gone under" that "he is either dead or teaching A B C." The father of Aeschines the orator kept such a school, and Demosthenes taunts the son with having to prepare the ink and sponge the forms and sweep the waiting-room.

To such a school Lysimachus will march unwillingly in the very early morning; at sunrise, in fact. His father will pay the fees on the last day of every month. There will be occasional school-festivals in honour of the Muses or of Hermes, the god of eloquence, at which the pupils will contribute towards a sacrifice and an entertainment. There will also be holidays, particularly in the early spring. It is interesting to know from Theophrastus that there were very mean men at Athens, and of a type of these he says " He is the sort of man not to send his children to school when it is the Festival of the

FIG. 53.—School scene: vase by Duris.

Muses, but to say they are unwell, so that they may avoid subscribing." The avaricious man also, "when his sons, through illness, do not go to school all the month, is the sort of man to deduct from the fee in proportion."

The boy can now read and write. He is next made to read the poets, particularly Homer, and to learn passages, if not the whole, by heart. While reciting them, the pupil stands up and delivers with intelligence and expression. His master sits in the chair, which was called *cathedra*, and which has given vogue to our expression *ex cathedra* for the dogmatic utterances of a master.

We are fortunate in possessing an illustration of the whole business from an Attic vase of the painter Duris. In the first of the two scenes, one boy is singing to the flute, another is having an exercise corrected: in the second scene, one youth is learning the fingering of the lyre, another is repeating verse: in both cases the paedagogus is seated on the right, keeping watch.

FIG. 54.—School scene: vase by Duris.

In Xenophon a character remarks that he "can still repeat all the *Iliad* and *Odyssey* by heart." The aim of all this, be it observed, is to cultivate the character by the familiar contemplation of great examples and high deliverances.

Next his musical education begins, generally about the thirteenth year. To the Greeks the musical education for a gentleman means singing and playing upon the lyre. The flute or clarionet is commonly left to professionals, for not only does it distort the face, it is also too orgiastic. For, strange as it may appear to this enlightened age, the chief aim of musical teaching at Athens was the proper cultivation of the feelings. Of course it was socially agreeable to be able to play and sing, but, chiefly, the effect sought was an effect on manners and conduct. There was no intention of turning out professionals, but of edifying the inner man. Side by side with playing upon the lyre the pupils appropriately read and learned lyric poetry.

Meanwhile his physical training has proceeded, under special teachers, in what were known as the wrestling-schools, the chief exercises as yet being in wrestling, running, and leaping. Almost all boys learned to dance and to swim. It may be remarked that the master in physical culture used the whip or the cane without stint, and while an adult Athenian citizen regarded it as an intolerable outrage to be struck or assaulted, he took all this corporal chastisement in his young days as a matter of course.

At about sixteen education in the ordinary sense is over. For boys of the poorer classes their work now begins, if it has not begun long ago. Those better circumstanced mostly proceed for two years more to something which corresponds to our Arts course at the University, combined with a severe course of gymnastics. The old tutor-slave is dispensed with, and they betake themselves, on the one hand to professors of rhetoric and general culture, on the other to trainers in wrestling, boxing, spear-throwing, and, in many cases, riding. We hear of fees of £40 — equal to £100 or more to-day — as payment for a full course in practical eloquence; and we also hear of poor men who, like the Scotch or American student, would work for hire in mills or elsewhere at nights in order to obtain the means to attend philosophic instruction in the daytime.

Two years pass in this way and Lysimachus is of age. He can read and write, sing and dance, play upon the lyre, swim,

Fig. 55. — Discobolus of Myron.

ride, wrestle, box, run, and leap; he can understand and quote Homer, Hesiod, and the lyric poets.   He knows how to carry himself in all sorts of societies. He is what was called *kalos kagathos*, "a fine and good" stamp of man.

Being first enrolled as a citizen on the records, he is called upon to undergo his military training. Along with all other young men of the same year — who may perhaps number about a thousand — he is marched to a temple, where he takes an oath that he will not disgrace his arms or desert his comrades in battle, and that he will obey orders, keep the laws and assist in their being kept, and defend and honour the shrines.   Clad in a regulation mantle and hat he becomes a probationary soldier. He is marched down to the harbour-town of Piraeus, where he serves in garrison duty, receiving 6d. a day (perhaps we may call it 1s. 3d.), and messing with perhaps a hundred others of his tribe.   Here he is under careful moral supervision, and is drilled and trained in the use of weapons, being apparently meanwhile considerably knocked about.   He is then marched back to Athens, where an assembly is held in the great theatre; he goes through his exercises, is presented with a spear and shield, and is sent to patrol the frontiers, receiving instruction in marching, digging trenches, fortifying and conducting siege-works.

Then he returns to Athens to do as he will, generally to sow a considerable amount of wild oats, but a highly capable man and a highly interesting one.

CHAPTER X

ARMY AND NAVY

CHAPTER X

ARMY AND NAVY

OUR Athenian is liable to military service from the age of eighteen to sixty, although men over fifty will hardly be called out except in the last resort. He has learned his drill between the ages of eighteen and twenty, including all the simple forming of line, wheeling, forming column, hollow square, and the like. There is nothing which can be justly called a "standing" army. But war-time comes — indeed it was pretty nearly always coming — and Lysimachus, going down to the market-place, finds a notice posted on a white board to the effect that all men on the roll up to the age of thirty are to muster in the Agora, or in the precincts of some temple, or at the theatre, perhaps the day after to-morrow, and that they are to bring their weapons and armour, together with a supply of food for three days. There was no free commissariat in the Athenian army. The infantryman receives daily pay from two obols, or a silver threepenny-piece, in the lowest cases, up to a drachma, or silver franc, in the highest. Out of this he is expected to buy his own supplies, and, since Greek campaigning distances are very short, a stock for three days is considered enough to begin with. The ordinary rank-and-file will put in their knapsacks a packet of meal, some salt, and a supply of onions and garlic.

A man of average means serves as a heavy-armed infantry-man. He wears no particular uniform, but must possess a set of armour, which he supplies for himself, and which may differ

Fig. 56. — Greek soldier and Persian.

a good deal from that of the next man in the ranks. This includes padded bronze greaves on the legs, a corselet or breastplate consisting of leather plated with bronze, a bronze

shield, round or oval, and a bronze helmet, with a neck-piece and short movable cheek-pieces and adorned with a plume or crest, and sometimes with two.
From the waist a leather garment is worn, falling in a fringe of thongs over the hips, to protect the lower portion of the body. The corselet, in two

FIG. 57.—Helmets, from coins.

halves, which are laced together in front and possess flaps coming over the shoulders, is put above this, and a plated belt goes round and braces the whole together. By his left side he

FIG. 58.—Putting on corselet: warriors arming.

wears a short sword, and in his right hand is a long lance of ashwood tipped with steel.

The Outlanders also could be called upon to serve in this style, and, including these, Athens could perhaps at a pinch turn out 20,000 such men as those described. But, besides, there are the persons too poor to supply such an equipment, and these are satisfied with a light shield, often of wood or wickerwork, a sword, and a javelin; or they may keep in the rear, armed with no shield at all, but simply with bow and arrows, sling, or light spear. A few cavalry, perhaps a thousand, complete the army. These are men well-to-do, who can supply and manage their own horse but are allowed a franc a day.

Fig. 59. — Armourer: Thetis receiving the weapons of Achilles.

Unhappily, during the latter portion of our period, the Athenians had begun to engage mercenaries to do their fighting, and this was with them, as everywhere, the beginning of the end.

Well, Lysimachus is in the heavy-armed infantry. He will not find the discipline very strict, according to our notions. But to fail to put in an appearance, to desert his post, or to show cowardice, meant that he was liable to a prosecution which might disgrace him and strip him of all his citizen rights.

We need not follow him into the details of a battle. When he meets the enemy he will probably form one of a line eight deep, he will hear the trumpet sound the charge, he will rush forward at the double with a cheer, and — let us hope he will get safely back to Athens in due time.

FIG. 60. — Armed soldier: the parting cup.

.   .   .   .   .   .

But the chief strength of Athens lies in her navy. She possesses in the docks at Peiraeus between 300 and 400 of those ships of war which perhaps might better be called galleys. They are about 120 or 130 feet

FIG. 61. — Trireme, from a relief.

long, about 17 wide, and have a draught of 6 or 7 feet. The propulsion of these vessels is chiefly by rowing.

There is, it is true, a mainmast with one large and one small square sail, and also a foremast with a small sail, but these will be removed before a battle, and in voyaging are mainly regarded as accessories. Such ships are built for speed, and, from their structure, are sometimes called "long" ships. They are easily drawn up on land or up slips into the ship-houses. Being propelled by oarsmen who sit in three tiers obliquely one slightly above another, their common name is "three-bankers." Other vessels, of one, two, four, and five banks, are met with, but are rare. When turned out in readiness for war, a three-banker's crew amounts to about 200 men, of whom 174 are oarsmen, ten or a dozen are marines, who are to fight in full armour on the deck, and the rest are boatswain and petty officers, a first officer (or "officer of the foredeck"), a steersman or navigating officer, the commander, and a few sailors to manage the tackling. When fully manned and strained to its utmost, the navy will thus require over 50,000 men to serve at the oars alone, and, since no large proportion of these can be citizens, and since the work is heavy, Outlanders, hired mercenaries, and even slaves are employed and paid by the state. The officers and marines are of course citizens. If citizens are ordered to row, they must perform the duty; but in such cases they would generally serve in the topmost tier, to which higher pay was attached, inasmuch as the oars were longer and the best men were required in that row. The average pay for the whole ship is three obols — perhaps equal in purchasing power to one shilling of our money — per man per day. It will be well to give here an illustration of the rowers on their seats, according to the common, but rather doubtful, theory. One tier is placed two feet lower than the next and one foot in front of it, and, when the men pull, those in the lower row fall back between the knees of those in the higher. The boatswain sets the time, and a flute helps and inspirits the men to keep it. The time of stroke and recovery are marked with the cries *op*, *ó-óp*, and the boatswain will now and again give the order to "lay on" or "put into it." The men themselves have also a sort of "yo-heave-oo" in the shape of "*rhup-pa-pai*." When speed is required in action or for

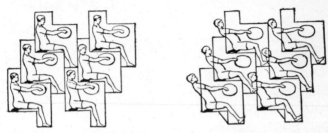

Fig. 62. — Rowers (conjectural).

flight, the whole 174 are at work ; on an ordinary voyage each tier is divided into three watches, and these take the rowing in turns.

At the stern of the vessel is a raised quarter-deck with officers' cabin and flagstaff. Behind the bows is another raised deck, and from under them, just beneath the water, there projects a mass of sharp timber shod with iron or bronze, with which the enemy's vessel is to be rammed and sunk. A favourite Athenian manœuvre is to charge full speed along an enemy's ship, draw in the oars on that side, crash through the enemy's oars and break them off short, then make a circle and ram her in the stern or the unprotected side.

Now it happens that our friend Pasicles may become

"commander" of such ship in spite of himself. He is a man of means, and he will at some time find himself called upon to undertake one of those "public burdens" which take the place of direct taxation. The state possesses a ship and rigging in the dock; it provides and pays the crews; but beyond this Pasicles — whose turn on the roster has come — finds himself, either alone or in a syndicate of others, put to the expense of getting the ship ready for sea, of keeping it for a year or other period in good repair, and of handing it and its rigging over at the end of that time in good order and condition. That is one way of seeing to the efficiency of the navy. There is a Dock-yard Board which looks sharply after these duties, and Pasicles bears his burden as a matter of course and looks as cheerful as possible. His title is "commander of a three-banker," although in all matters of mere navigation he is of course guided by the sailing-master, and in matters of war by the orders and signals of his admiral. And so engaged, we will leave him.

CHAPTER XI

RELIGION

CHAPTER XI

RELIGION

IT is time now to look at the religious side of Athenian life.

A clear and accurate description of Athenian religion would hardly be a possibility, even if volumes were devoted to the subject. In a sketch like ours we must be satisfied if we can state fairly its general character and its chief phenomena. If the representative Athenian had possessed any definite notion of the precise number of the gods, or of their functions and relations to each other, or of the principles upon which they acted in dealing with mankind or letting mankind alone, then our task would be easier. But in point of fact classical Athens had no formulated theology; it learned no express creed; it possessed nothing corresponding to our Church, or Bible, or Catechism, or preachers, or Doctors of Divinity. And even if it had possessed these, there would still remain the question how far the state enforced the recognised doctrines, how far individuals really accepted them, and to what extent, if they acknowledged the theory, they carried it into practice.

Even for our own day we should find it difficult to be very positive as to the exact nature and reality of religious belief around us. We have the sincere and practical religious believer, the man who perfunctorily assents to a religious system and its ceremonies, the merely superstitious man, the thoughtful and conscientious doubter, the indifferentist, and the more or less aggressive atheist. During the Athenian period which we are considering you might have found each and all of these, and the only one who ran into any danger was the aggressive or obstreperous person who interfered with the beliefs and practices of others. His conduct, at least, was palpably anti-social.

If we superficially survey what is known as Greek mythology, and do not distinguish the Homeric world from the Athenian world, nor Plato from the Athenian man in the street, we shall naturally be amazed at the intellectual and moral inconsistency which appears in the religion of men so keen-witted as the people of Athens. Do our friends Pasicles and Lysimachus really believe in all those male and female deities of Lemprière's Dictionary, with all the flagrant failings and passions which the contradictory legends attribute to them? Does any power insist that they shall believe, or pretend to believe, in them? And how does such a confused and unworthy theology come to exist? And how does it operate on conduct?

Let us attempt a succinct answer to these questions, though not in the same order. And, first, let us premise that a vast deal which appears in the dictionaries of mythology as " Greek " was practically unknown at Athens. Nevertheless, keeping to that part which does apply, we must begin by admitting that the religious condition of classical Athens did undoubtedly lag behind its intellect and its social civilisation. Nothing is so conservative as an inherited religion, and the religion of Athens was an inheritance. We have already observed that the classical Greek was the outcome of a blending of northern invaders, akin to the Teutons and Celts, with earlier denizens of the country, who were of a quite alien Mediterranean stock. Greek religion was equally the outcome of a blending of the two. Hence many of its inconsistent and even incompatible elements. In religious matters the average mind shrinks from inquiry or logical scrutiny until the last possible moment. Here we have two early races, one directing its thoughts and worship chiefly, though not solely, to powerful and comparatively genial beings in the skies, with nothing uncanny about them, but with a set of good robust human virtues and human vices; the other turning its worship chiefly to powerful but ungenial beings of the earth or underneath it, and endowed with distinctly mysterious and uncanny natures and attributes. Combine these two stocks, interpenetrate and confuse these beliefs, as they pass with the generations from parents to children and from nurses to their charges, and you get, not only a set of deities in a world aloft, or " Olympus," and a set of daemonic agencies acting from an underground world or " Hades," but also a hopeless confusion of their names and functions. Date it all from that very early time when man had no scientific understanding of the operations of nature, of the manner in which the sun rose or the buds appeared in the spring, or of the reason why wine intoxicates or diseases come, or why there is thunder or earthquake, and when they consequently invented divine agencies and concocted legends more or less ingenious to explain such things. Next imagine such divine agencies becoming more and more personified, and the legends more and more elaborated and poetised, but nowhere any systematic list of gods or of their precise powers, or of the legends which one ought to believe concerning each.

As refinement of society and intellect proceeds, the sculptor and painter step in, and the outward representations of the higher or more beneficent divinities grow into majesty and beauty, while the lower and malevolent agencies are made correspondingly unlovely, unless they are kept in the background altogether. Now take an Athenian child, who begins by listening to the "old wives' tales" of his nurse; then is present at domestic rites and sacrifices, which impress him without his understanding them; afterwards learns his old-fashioned Homer and his poets, before he has any notion of questioning their theology; next moves about among altars and splendid temples and statues of Zeus, Athena, Dionysus, and many another divinity; is later on initiated into awesome mysteries, which are addressed to his emotions and not to his reason; and is at all times trained to undertake no enterprise, public or private, without first consulting the will of the gods, praying to them, and sacrificing to them.

There we have the situation of our friends Pasicles and Lysimachus. To their religious condition there have contributed the effects of legends, poetry, and ceremonies in childhood, and of public practices, art and ritual in maturity. But, being reasonable men, they will practically discredit the absurd and immoral elements in mythology; they will believe that the Olympian gods are as just and wise as they are powerful; they will laugh at the grosser superstitions of fear; but they will, nevertheless, perform their rites and ceremonies, whether to the gods above or to the powers below, with all decorum and without question. To them Zeus will, in a general way, represent a real all-ruler, Athena a real goddess of arts and wisdom, who specially protects the city of Athens, Poseidon a real power controlling the sea and causing earthquakes. Of these and other deities their conception will be approximately that which the artists have embodied in their statues or which painters have depicted on walls or on vases. They will believe that the spirits of the dead live in the under-world a dull and unenviable existence, which is a dim copy of life on earth; that the very impious are punished there in "Tartarus," a deep place of torment; and that the very pious enjoy a special and more attractive abode in the Elysian fields. They will pay respect to the departed, who are still very able, and ready, to make or mar in human life.

We may take these two citizens as representing the typical or middle point in Athenian religion. On opposite sides of them lie two other classes of persons. On the one side are the ignorant and vulgar, or the constitutionally superstitious. To these all the legends are credible, simply because they exist. Not only do they not question the actual existence of the gods; they do not pretend to select, nor to exercise any reason in respect of details. Moreover they have a distinct leaning to the uncanny side of religion ; the more strange or secret its ceremonies, the more corybantic or emotional, the better they like them; they see omens and daemonic influences everywhere ; they are always consulting soothsayers — at threepence a consultation — or performing rites of exorcism. Meanwhile on the other side are the thinkers, whether professed philosophers, poets, or simply vigorous reasoners. In the minds of these there are the gravest doubts as to who the gods are, how many they are, whether they exist at all, and to what extent they interfere with human action. They are in doubt as to the under-world, as to whether death is a perpetual sleep, or complete annihilation, or an after-life. Some of them are practically monotheists ; some are disbelievers in the intervention of the gods in human affairs; but, all alike, these will have it that, if gods there are, they are not the faulty human divinities of the old women's tales, or of Homer. These men often know something of physical philosophy; they can explain some phenomena of nature and guess at others. They are the sceptics, agnostics, and freethinkers of the day, and their numbers are certainly not inconsiderable.

But we are concerned with the average representative Athenian, and to him we will confine ourselves.

Pasicles would tell you that in the vague aloft there are certain deities, male and female, who are to be honoured with temples and sacrifices and prayers in return for their favours and services to mankind; and of these he will, like any Greek, name first and foremost Zeus. Being an Athenian, he will name in the second place Athena. But there is a long list of others — Apollo, Dionysus, Poseidon, Aphrodite, and so on — some more prominent, some less so, and some hardly considered at all. He will next tell you, though with less willingness, that there are powers of the earth, who are apt to be jealous and vengeful, and whom he soothes with offerings on special days, but to whom he does not build temples or erect statues. If you ask him why he worships the upper gods, he will say frankly that he desires to gain their help and favour in the way of health, wealth, success, and happiness. If you ask him why he makes offerings to the lower powers and deities, he will reply that it is because they demand such things, and to neglect them is to run the risk of dire visitations in mind, body, or estate.

If you watch him praying, you will see that to the upper gods he brings a victim of white colour; that in prayer he lifts his face and the palms of his hands with some appearance of brightness and confidence; that if he burns a portion of the sacrifice upon the altar he makes a feast upon the rest; whereas to the lower gods he bends his face and hands earthward in gloom, and of the victim — which in this case is black — he will touch nothing, but leave it to be wholly consumed. To the Olympian gods he will sacrifice in the morning; to the nether gods it will be towards evening.

He does not know that he is the product of a gradual mixture of two old religions, one a worship of the powers of nature and their personifications, the other a worship of ancestors and their ghosts.

In the next place, what relation is there between his worship of the gods and his moral conduct? Almost none. So long as his behaviour to the superhuman powers is ceremonially correct, that is to say, so long as he performs his prayers and sacrifices, joins in the festivals, and comports himself reverently when mentioning the deities, or when in their sacred precincts, he is fulfilling all the duties demanded by religion. His moral conduct is determined by the laws of the land and the tradition of society, not by any code of divine ordinances. Lysimachus does not ask, "What does Zeus or Athena command?" but "What does the law command? What did my parents have me taught? What will Pasicles think?" In other words, sound morality is a social virtue rather than a religious virtue. It is quite true that, according to the higher minds of Athens, Zeus punished the man who broke an oath or violated manifest natural claims; it is also true that to those better minds the gods looked with favour on the man of pure hands and conscience; but, after all, the actual standard of purity,

P

whether of hand or conscience, was the standard erected by society and the law, not an ideal standard known by revelation. The gods were the protectors of human relations, not original fountains of abstract morality. The fact is that the better Athenian minds were trying their best to bring the prehistoric gods up to the higher standard of the morality of themselves, which had been evolved by their civilisation. So true is it that "man makes gods in his own image."

Meanwhile our average respectable citizen looked to his fellowmen to dictate and judge his morality. The gods would be satisfied with a proper degree of respect, and, for anything beyond the minimum of such respect, our citizen looked for a *quid pro quo* in the shape of direct favours.

We may, of course, suppose that no Athenian could climb the steps of the Acropolis, pass through its majestic Propylaea, survey and enter the splendid and impressive Parthenon, and gaze upon the colossal statue of the Maiden Goddess, without feeling that it must be his best self that approached so august a deity. But his best self meant something which was not to be found in any inspired Bible, nor was delivered to the emotions by any body of preachers, but which was set forth by the laws and by good form. There never were minds more free from the anguish of moral yearnings, or ideals of self-mortification, than those of classical Athens.

It is in keeping with this attitude that religion at Athens was made a matter of state and put under the general supervision of an officer elected annually. There was no such thing as an established Church or an organised priesthood. There were simply independent temples, altars, and festivals of a number of gods, each of whom had his appointed minister or ministers, whose concern it was to conduct his sacrifices, direct his festivals, look after his temple, and guard his property. Some of these ministers (if we use the word "priest" it may be misleading, since he was rather a public officer of a comparatively lay character) were hereditary, some were specially elected by the people, some were chosen by lot, whether for life or for a term. The only necessary qualifications were that the minister should be of unblemished body and character; otherwise he would be unwelcome to the god whom he was to serve. He would have to understand the ritual belonging to particular shrines and occasions, but he received no special training beyond this. There was no theology, no preaching. He was not a clergyman, had no cure of souls, no parish, no duty of moral instruction or similar responsibility. He had also nothing to do with the minister of any other god or shrine. The ministers were, moreover, of both sexes, and in most cases celibacy was not required of either. They were public officers, and, as such, enjoyed a respect which was naturally increased by their association with the god. At the larger temples the priest or priestess — as we may now venture to call them without misunderstanding — was furnished with slaves or servants, who were paid by the state, or from endowments, to sweep the buildings, act as beadles, make proclamations, play flute accompaniments, and lend other help. Besides these, it was the practice at the more important ceremonies to call in as acolytes a number of boys and girls of good parentage and character, and distinguished for appearance and bearing; to be one of the selected for such an occasion was regarded as an honour to both the acolyte and the parents.

The emoluments of the priest or priestess consisted of gifts, often valuable, together with such perishable edibles as fruits and confections which had been offered to the god, as well as certain understood parts of all burnt sacrifices. In some cases free maintenance was given in the City-hall and a special house was provided. Yet most Athenian priests and priestesses must have been independent of these material emoluments. What chiefly attracted them to the office was the distinction and respect which belonged to it. They enjoyed, for example, a seat of honour at the theatre and at other festive gatherings. At such times they were marked by their long hair, their flowing white robe, and their wreath, which was made of the plant sacred to the particular deity, as the olive was to Athena, the laurel to Apollo, and the ivy to Dionysus.

There were, however, other religious ceremonies than those of particular temples. These belonged to clans, families, or individual houses. Apart from all this, the typical house had its own altar to Zeus in the court, and its special household deities. To these it was no priest, but the house-father, Pasicles himself, who sacrificed. The case was very much like that of the British house-father conducting family prayers, or the ship's captain taking the place of a chaplain. But there is this difference, that at Athens there was no such thing as ordination, and the line was not drawn as between priest and layman, but as between public officiator and private officiator.

And here perhaps we ought to describe a sacrifice, or what we should call religious service, at a temple. We have already given some description of a temple itself and of its structure. A burnt sacrifice, however, takes place at an altar outside the building, and this for obvious reasons. Altars were of various shapes, sizes, and material. In the country you might build one of turf or rough stones; in the city they were naturally of marble. Before a temple the altar stands in such a position that, when the doors are opened, the statue of the deity, which

FIG. 63. — Sacrifice of a pig.

regularly faces east, is looking towards it, while the votaries on their part can look towards the statue (see p. 45).

The participants approach the altar in festal attire and with wreaths upon their heads; a brand is taken from the fire and dipped in water, and with this the company is sprinkled. The minister exclaims "beware of your words," or "keep silence," and prayers are then offered with uplifted head and hand and uttered in a distinct and audible voice. Sometimes there is chanted an ode specially composed. The victim, such as a sheep or an ox, or several (according to the occasion), is led to the altar, and its demeanour observed. If it does not struggle back, the indication is good. Barley-grains are scattered on its head; the throat is cut so that the blood shoots into the flame; the company raises a jubilant shout; the animal is deftly skinned and carved; the thigh-bones, covered with fat, or else the lower part of the chine, are burned in the fire, so that the savour mounts to heaven; and the rest of the meat — except the portion for the officiating priest — becomes a feast for the participants, many of whom perhaps hardly ever taste meat except on such occasions. The conduct of the sacrifice is accompanied by music from the flute, while prognostications are drawn from the way in which the fire and smoke ascend, and also from an examination of the entrails of the victim.

About Greek prayer there is nothing mystic. It is not a prayer for a pure heart and for inward light, but for some definite outward help or blessing or success, for victory in war, or freedom from plague, or the like. A private individual prays for prosperity in a journey or other enterprise. He is generally quite definite, and therefore unlike Socrates, who stood alone when he prayed simply for "good" and left it to the gods to decide what was good. It was a point of religious etiquette to utter the prayer distinctly, so that it might be known to contain nothing unfair or improper. Commonly a promise or vow was attached; the god was in fact guaranteed a *quid pro quo*. The prayer for rain ran merely "Rain, rain, dear Zeus, on the fields and plains of the Athenians."

Apart from such larger sacrifices, inside the temple a table stood in front of the statue, and on this the votaries might place flowers, fruits, loaves, cakes made like sacrificial animals, and the like. Vessels of gold and silver were offered in the temple, and were there kept around the shrine on stands, shelves, brackets, or on the floor, while outside in the vestibule, behind a railing, stood tripods and other large offerings which might more safely be exposed. There was hardly anything which an Athenian might not dedicate in a temple in token of his gratitude, whether cups of precious metal, or works of art, or captured armour, or simply the implements of a trade which he was abandoning. In the temple of Asclepius, the god of healing, it was common to affix to the walls models of arms, eyes, or limbs which his influence had cured.

It cannot be too much insisted upon that, indifferentists, philosophers, and higher minds apart, the populace of Athens was, as in the days of St. Paul, "too superstitious." The fact is particularly shown by their belief in a multitude of omens, their traffic in divination of all sorts, and their cultivation of occult and ecstatic ceremonies. The poets, the better orators, the philosophers, and other cultivated or hard-headed Athenians, might condemn the professional seers and dream-readers and corybantic "jumpers and shakers," but meanwhile an infinity of occurrences caused genuine worry to many an honest citizen. He might stumble as he went out of doors, or catch sight of some unlucky bird to his left hand; or, in the country, he might meet a hare; or he might have had a bad dream; or he might overhear some chance utterance which sounded in-auspicious. Thereupon he betakes himself to the professional interpreter of these things, and the seer gives him advice for a threepenny-piece. Anything from a sneeze to an eclipse called for its expiation. There is a chapter of Theophrastus concerning this type, and it is comforting to reflect that his choice of such a "Superstitious Man" as one of his character-studies is an indication that the type was a special one. "The superstitious man is the sort of man who . . . if a weasel runs across the way, will not proceed until some one has passed along, or until he has thrown three stones across the road . . . and if a mouse gnaws a hole in a bag of meal, he will go to the expounder and ask what he ought to do, and if he replies 'Give it to the cobbler to patch,' he will take no notice, but will turn away and offer expiations. . . . And when he has a dream, he is off to the dream-readers, the seers, and the augurs, to ask what god or goddess he should pray to. . . . On seeing a madman or a person in a fit he goes all of a shudder and spits into his bosom."

Nevertheless, though the professional diviners — the private practitioners of seership, so to speak — were discredited, the whole community accepted the authority of the great oracles or prophetic shrines like that at Delphi, and also sought initiation into what were known as the "Mysteries" of Eleusis. It would lie outside our province to deal with these. The only care we must take is to avoid speaking of them with impatient contempt. There can be little doubt that, with all its irrational proceedings, there was in the classical time nothing either vulgar or charlatan about the oracle of Delphi. There can be as little doubt that, amid all the emotional mummery of the Eleusinian mysteries, there was something almost sacramental ; and we must trust Aristotle when he says that the initiated

" learned nothing in particular, but received impressions, and were brought into a certain frame of mind."

It has already been observed that Athenian religion was a matter of state. The state was, however, peculiarly liberal-minded in this domain. It did not go out of its way to inquire into your private beliefs, nor compel you to any conformity therein. On the other side, you must not unduly meddle with the beliefs of your neighbour by preaching atheism or novel divinities of your own, and you must not damage or insult sacred property or sacred symbols, nor divulge or parody the mysteries, nor behave in an unseemly way at religious ceremonies or festivities.

If you did any of these things, you were liable to an action for " impiety " or " irreverence," and the power of the state to fine or imprison or banish you or put you to death with hemlock was theoretically large and vague. But in practice the state let you alone, until your conduct became, or was considered, markedly dangerous or anti-social. The question as to when it did become dangerous was decided by a jury of five hundred of your fellow-citizens.

Now let us remember that Athens, during all our period, was full of sophists, philosophers, and cultivated men, who argued about the gods and their character. According to Plato it was well known that some denied their existence, and others declared that at least they never intervened in human affairs. Let us remember also that the comic poet Aristophanes actually produces a deity like Dionysus on the stage, and places him in ridiculous and humiliating positions. And let us add that a prosecution for " impiety " was one of the very rarest in a state in which prosecuting or being prosecuted was almost an order of the day. It must be evident that the Athenians were in the highest degree tolerant or easy-going in the matter of religion. But when, on the other hand, we find Protagoras expelled from Athens because he put it in writing that "he had no means of learning whether the gods existed or not"; and Socrates condemned to death on a charge — among others — of " not recognising the gods whom the state recognised, and introducing another new set of divinities"; what are we to think? The answer is that these charges are only a use of legal machinery in order to get rid of men whose conduct and influence had rendered them unpopular and seemed to threaten the character of the community. Protagoras was a foreigner, and we need not consider him; but Socrates is a clear instance in point. The real charge against him is that he was a corrupter of the young, and, in fact, a public nuisance. Our notion of Socrates is that which has been presented to us by his pupils Plato and Xenophon, and they were probably excellent judges from an aristocratic point of view; but if we could discover the ordinary Athenian feeling towards him, we should find that it was one of prejudice and irritation, not so much at his religious heterodoxies, which were common enough, but at his whole personality and influence. In a small and clubbable community like Athens personal unpopularity counted for much, and the accusers of Socrates plainly seized the psychological moment.

CHAPTER XII

FESTIVALS AND THE THEATRE

CHAPTER XII

FESTIVALS AND THE THEATRE

THE religion of Pasicles and Lysimachus therefore sits easily upon them. And on the whole it is a cheerful and festive religion. It delights in holidays, processions, sports and feasts. The theatre at Athens, both tragic and comic, was the outcome of religion ; the great athletic games at Olympia and elsewhere were the outcome of religion. It is as with us ; almost all our holidays — such as Christmas and Easter — are in origin religious holidays. There were festivals to celebrate the budding spring and the autumn vintage, and these were parts of the worship of the gods of fructification, who pass under such names as Dionysus (or Bacchus) and Demeter. If there was once some gloomy day of celebrations to the dead — an "All Souls' Day" — it soon became converted into a joyous holiday, after the manner in which the solemn Good Friday is gradually coming to be treated by the generality. There were country festivities about Christmas time, a feast of the wine-press in January, an "All Souls'" festival of three days in February, a great "City Festival" of Bacchus for five days in March, a festival of first-fruits in May, the splendid holiday of Athena for six days in the July of every fourth year. There were other festivals scattered through the calendar.

Inasmuch as the two chief and most distinctive Athenian celebrations are the feast of Athena — the patron goddess — in each fourth year (a minor festival of the same deity being celebrated annually), and the feast of Dionysus with its theatrical performances every March, we may take a brief glance at the former and then deal somewhat more fully with the latter.

The "Panathenaea" included, in the first place, contests in athletics, in music, and in literary recitation. In the large and domed "Hall of Song" there was a public competition in the delivery of passages of Homer, another, in singing to the accompaniment of the harp, another in instrumental music upon the harp, or lyre, and the flute. The rewards were prizes in money, together with the outward distinction of a wreath or crown.

In the athletic competitions there were included running, jumping, wrestling, spear-throwing, discus-throwing, and a foot-race of men in full armour. In these events boys competed with boys, youths with youths, and men with men; the contests were conducted in heats, and the prize, which dated from early times, was a strange one. It consisted of a stock of olive oil of considerable marketable value, and of jars artistically painted. The reason for this was that the festival belonged to Athena, who was not only the goddess of Athens, but also of its special product, the olive. In another competition, very Athenian in character, each of the ten political divisions of the people presented four-and-twenty men, the finest in appearance and the best arrayed which it could produce, and a prize for what was styled "fine manhood" was awarded to the best set. Horse-racing and chariot-racing were great features of the meeting, and every inducement was held out to Athenians of means to breed horses and practise driving and horsemanship. But be it said in passing that classical Athens despised the professional athlete and pot-hunter, who, nevertheless, ultimately managed to ruin the competitions.

On another day there followed an all-night festivity of song and dance and of races with the torch, in which one chain of runners competed with another chain, the object being to pass a blazing torch along the line from point to point in the quickest time without permitting it to go out.

The chief day of all was the occasion of the greatest procession known in Athens. The citizens and Outlanders gathered in the Cerameicus, the cavalrymen on their horses, the public officers in all their regalia, and every one in his most brilliant attire. The main business is to escort to the Acropolis a large and gorgeous robe, to be presented to the ancient statue of Athena. This, which is of yellow material embroidered with legendary exploits of Athena against the Giants, is spread as a sail upon the mast of the model of a ship, which is propelled along the street on wheels or rollers. The cavalry in their bright cloaks ride ahead, the winners in the contests, wearing their wreaths, the dignitaries and old men of good repute, carrying olive branches, follow after. Then come maidens of good birth, bearing gracefully on their heads the light baskets used in the sacrifice; and behind them women of the Outlanders carrying the parasols and the camp-stools of the privileged daughters of Athens. The rest of the procession is made up of every citizen of Athens who is able to attend. From the Cerameicus the procession moves down through the public square, winds through the chief streets to the foot of the Acropolis, mounts through the Propylaea, and passes to the older temple, in front of which a great sacrifice — nominally of a hundred animals — is made. A feast follows, and the whole festival is closed by a regatta at the harbour-town of Peiraeus. Meanwhile all manner of side-shows, acrobatic tricks, conjuring tricks, sword-swallowing, and fire-swallowing, go on amid temporary booths and stalls corresponding to the structures erected at those English fairs which are now so rapidly dying out.

To us, however, the most interesting of Athenian festivities is the spring feast of Dionysus, the god of fructification of plants, and in particular of the vine; most interesting, both in itself and because it has left to us a magnificent legacy in the shape of the tragedies of Aeschylus, Sophocles, and Euripides, and the comedies of Aristophanes, which are not only such superlative works of literary art, but have so profoundly influenced the shape of our own dramatic creations. We need not describe the revels and deliberate intoxications of the feast in general. But the Attic theatre and its productions are an elaborate outcome of this blending of worship and revel, and we cannot afford to neglect so important and far-reaching an element in Athenian life.

There is no occasion here to discuss the manner in which the old rough dances and crude mimicry of the spring holiday grew into the extremely artistic drama of the classical period. We need only take the performances as they actually were, and briefly picture them.

But first we must be warned against a common error. It was only during the last part of our period that the great stone theatre of Athens was being built. When our friend Lysimachus was a youth, the theatre was a very different thing from what

FIG. 64. — Theatre at Athens (present).

it had become by the time he was an old man. The structure and staging of the theatre to which Pericles or Plato went, and for which Sophocles and Aristophanes wrote, was, like the theatre of Shakespeare, by no means on a level with the genius and poetry of the dramatist, or the merit of the acting, or the enthusiasm of the spectators. A temporary erection, with tiers of seats, was built round three parts of a flat circle; facing the seats, at the opposite side of the flat space, was perhaps a low wooden daïs, the first hint of a stage; behind this again a wooden structure, with a certain amount of scenery roughly indicated upon it or upon canvas hung in front of it, to represent a palace, a house of one or two stories, a cave, or whatever was required. As with the London theatre of Shakespeare's day, a good deal had to be left to the imagination of the spectators. It was hinted to the audience, both in words and in a few accessories, that they were in Thebes or Hades, and they were expected to believe it. But, as dramatic art and experience advanced on the technical side, more and more was done in the way of lending an air of reality. There were introduced a few mechanical contrivances and some imperfect devices for creating a change of scene — although Greek drama, for the most part, avoids such changes, mainly in view of the practical difficulty. Let us, for our purposes, suppose those advances to have been made, and in place of the old wooden theatre, let us imagine that we are at the date — contemporary with Demosthenes or Aristotle — when there was in existence the immense stone structure of which remains have been unearthed. That building will accommodate, or at least will hold closely packed, nearly 30,000 spectators, and yet the actor's voice will be heard distinctly in the topmost row. From a glance at the plan upon the chart of Athens, and then at a drawing of the existing remains, it is possible to get a far better idea than words can impart of the theatre of Athens, as the seats rose in an irregular curve of about two-thirds of a circle up the side of the Acropolis hill. Some of the upper seats were actually cut in the rock itself. The theatre, which has no

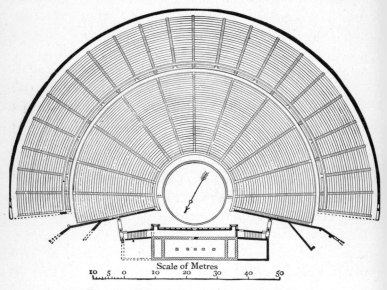

Fig. 65.— Typical plan of theatre (Epidaurus).

roof, faces south, in order to catch the warmth, the season for the performances being early spring. To supplement the notion thus formed, we may take a scheme, not indeed of this actual theatre, but one sufficiently illustrating the type. In the actual remains, as here drawn, there is something which does not belong to our period, but for which it is the Roman of centuries later who is responsible. The steep wall round the dancing-place should not be there, but the slope of the seats should be carried right down in a much more graceful way, as depicted in the next illustration, where the wall *c* should be removed.

The seats were made as easy as stone would admit by hollowing the surface and under the front. It was, however, a common thing to have your own cushion brought along. The chairs which appear in the front row are for the use of the priests of certain special deities and for the highest officers of

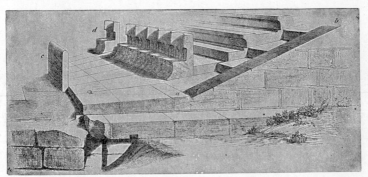

Fig. 66. — Seats sloping to orchestra.

state. The middle seat, which is covered with figures carved in relief, is naturally that of the priest of Dionysus, who is the god of the festivity. The stage at this period is not a fixture, and is of no great height. Somewhere in good view of the audience stand bronze statues of the great dramatists of the past.

So much for the building. As for the performance, be it remembered that the occasion is one of religion, and that the whole state owns the theatre and is the supreme director of the proceedings. Moreover it must be premised that, while the

FIG. 67. — Seat of priest of Dionysus.

performances are for the delight of the spectators, they are also contests for a prize between rival dramatists and rival actors. There is no private speculation about the matter. There are to be, on three days, three sets of tragedies by three composers, and a comedy by each of five composers; and the state, through the proper officer, will begin by selecting, a sufficient time beforehand, the playwrights who seem likely to present the best work.   It will then assign to each by lot a chief or " star " actor out of a recognised list, and that actor will choose the second and third, who are to support him; for, however many characters (except supers) may nominally appear in a play, their parts must generally be so arranged that three actors can between them perform them all.   These actors will be paid by the state.   This appeared to the Athenians better policy than for a play to be acted by a cast with a weak "tail."

Next, the proper officer assigns to each playwright, out of a roster, a person of means, whose turn it is to undertake such burden.   This citizen will hire, dress, and train a body of singers and dancers — fifteen for tragedy, twenty-four for comedy — who take a part in the play under the name of the " chorus."   In this sense it is the state which meets the expense.

A Greek drama is practically a compound of dialogue and acting with opera and artistic dance.   The words and the play are the first thing, and these must be literature; the music and dancing come next; while the staging is of comparatively little moment.   Hence it was necessary that every participator should be trained to the highest degree of perfection in both voice and movement.   The first requirement of an Athenian actor was command of a clear, flexible, and sonorous voice; the chorus must be prepared to execute its music and evolutions with the utmost precision.

Well, the training is done, and the first day arrives.   At daybreak the spectators — men, women, and boys — come streaming into the theatre, partly through the passages at the side of the stage, and partly through two entrances near the upper rows. They may bring cushions with them, and they will also frequently bring light refreshments. It is etiquette to wear a garland of ivy-leaves and festive attire. The first chairs will be occupied by the dignitaries already mentioned: other front seats will be given to foreign envoys, to citizens specially honoured for some service to their country, and to victors in the great Grecian games. According to Theophrastus, the "Man of Petty Ambitions" — the "Snob," in fact — is always anxious to secure a seat near the high officials. As distinguished or popular persons enter, the audience will applaud or cheer them; unpopular persons may be greeted by whistling and clucking. Special sections of the theatre are set apart for the council of 500, for the women, for the youths serving their conscription, and for foreigners. Officials carrying wands are posted to carry out such arrangements in orderly fashion and, presumably, to make the audience sit close.

Thus just after daybreak everything is ready. The whole morning will be occupied by one set of tragedies. Comedy will follow in the afternoon after lunch. To-morrow, another set of tragedies in the morning, other comedy in the afternoon; and so for the third day. Remember that such a festival takes place only once in the year, and that even comedies are only seen twice or at most thrice annually. After a few ceremonies, which do not here concern us, the crier proclaims that the tragic poet So-and-So will "bring in his chorus," and the performance begins. On the level floor moves the chorus; on the low stage, or on the level itself, are the actors; and merciless in its criticism is the audience in the seats. The performers, be it premised, are all men. If the piece is strong and good, the language and the thoughts noble, and if the actor is effective, the spectators yield themselves up freely to the pathos and excitement, the feelings of pity and fear aroused by the piece. They will be hushed in profound silence, or they will weep and start up and sway themselves about when the action reaches its climax. They applaud by clapping their hands, and occasionally they shout the Greek equivalent of "encore." But, if the piece is poor, they whistle, cluck with their tongues, kick their heels against the seats, and drive it from the stage. To use their own words, they "throw it out." If the piece is simply indifferent, they bring out their refreshments and go on eating their fruit or confectionery and drinking their wine. If they greatly disapprove of an actor, they not only whistle and cluck, but in extreme cases they pelt him with figs, nuts, grapes, or olives. This must have been done to a far less extent in the great Athenian theatre than in the smaller ones in the country. Aeschines, the orator, was once a third-rate actor, and Demosthenes declared that, when playing in the country, he was so pelted with figs and such things that he collected enough to set up a fruit-shop. Even stones were not unknown as missiles at some performances, though this would not occur at our tragedy. Once an inferior musician, who desired to repair a house, went to a friend to borrow stones for the purpose, promising that he would pay them back out of "the receipts of his next performance." Also a comic playwright once came into the theatre with his cloak full of stones, and himself threw them down for the subsequent use of his audience.

And here it is necessary to say that the taste of the Athenian audience was in the main right. A certain number of repre-sentative citizens was first selected; ten of these were then drawn by lot and made judges of the plays and actors; and when the ten had deposited their several verdicts in a receptacle for the purpose, the first five drawn from this receptacle decided the prizes. This should be a fairly adequate way of getting at the opinion of the average intelligent man, and it was this opinion which awarded the prize to an Aeschylus, a Sophocles, a Euripides, or an Aristophanes. The judgment of a special clique or *coterie* of illuminati is scarcely ever right; the opinion of humanity at large is not always right, but history shows that it is more to be trusted. Aristotle indeed complains that in his day the audience had a weakness for poetic justice, that it had too much of the melodramatic instinct for the triumph of virtue and the discomfiture of vice. The gallery "gods" in the Athenian theatre were numerous, and like the gallery gods elsewhere, they had a taste for fine moral sen-timents delivered with an air. Nevertheless the judgment of the audience as a whole was in the classical time remarkably true. Yet then, as now, there was always the superior person who, according to Theophrastus, made a point of hissing when the rest applauded and of clapping when they were silent.

The scenery, it has been remarked, was scanty, although wood painted in perspective was already employed. One way of assisting a change was by means of two small triangular structures, one at either end of the stage, with painting on each of the three sides. These could be turned round on a pivot, and to that extent the scene was shifted. For the most part all changes and operations were within view of the audience, who took them for granted, as they did in the Globe Theatre of Shakespeare. If a god had to appear from the sky he was swung by a crane, specially called the "machine," on to an elevated platform, or balcony, called the "god-stage"; and, since he was too often called in to solve a difficulty in the plot, the expression "the god from the machine (*deus ex machina*)" is to this day proverbial for such miraculous intervention. But, as in the Shakespearian theatre, defects in scenic equipment were atoned for by great literature and powerful acting. Also, as in the Shakespearian theatre, the dressing of both actors and chorus was magnificent and costly.

FIG. 68. — Tragic actor; ivory.

Doubtless to a close view a tragic actor in full dress was an amazing sight. Remember the vast size of the auditorium, remember that the details of facial expression on the stage were necessarily imperceptible to the majority, and that there were no such things as opera-glasses; then perhaps it is intelligible why, under those gorgeous robes, a tragic actor had padded his person, why he walked in boots lifted on several inches of cork sole, and why, completely covering his head, he wore a mask, which he could change either when assuming another character, or when he was to be represented as having undergone affliction or sickness. In the distance, on the stage, the crudeness of all this equipment is toned down, and, just as scene-painting looks finished and right when seen from the right point of view, and would look wrong if too finished, so was it with the Athenian actor's appearance. But there must meanwhile be no lack of finish about his voice. He

FIG. 69. — Tragic masks; from a painting.

must not rant or bellow, and his articulation and intonation are judged by the finest and most scrupulous ear ever possessed by an audience. A slip in accent or pronunciation evokes shouts of ridicule, and he never hears the last of it. Also he must not over-act; that is called "acting the monkey."

Meanwhile the chorus, led by its head-man (from whom we derive our term "coryphaeus"), from time to time sings and dances to a flute accompaniment. The singing is in unison, since arrangement in harmony is as yet unknown; and, first and foremost, the words must be heard distinctly. The dancing is not our dancing. It is not primarily a matter of the feet. There

FIG. 70. — Mask of Perseus.

are, of course, graceful and elegant movements to and fro; but Athenian dancing was done with the whole body; the head, hands, and every part are made expressive; the gestures and motions are expressive; they mean something, and are an appropriate emphasis to the words. And, sad to say, all the time there is a man in the audience who is fast asleep, and who will only wake up to find the theatre empty.

At noon the first set of tragedies is over. There is an interval for lunch, and in the afternoon the seats are again packed for the comic performance. The only difference is that women who respect themselves will stay at home. The .wit and humour of the Athenian comedians were in the highest degree brilliant. Aristophanes, for example, is the most com-

Fig. 71. — Comic masks; from a painting.

prehensive blend of Molière, Sheridan, Gilbert and Sullivan, and farce. But the fun is far too uproarious and the tone far too unrestrained for the Athenian matron.

In the method of performance there is no essential difference; the difference lies only in the purpose. The audience comes to laugh. It is a festival of Dionysus, and whether persons or classes of persons are satirised, it is best to take everything in good part.

Fig. 72. — Lysicrates' monument.

For three days the performances continue, and for a year afterwards the audience will have upon their lips quotations from the tragedies and jokes from the comedies; they will be humming snatches from the choruses; they will be striking attitudes in imitation of the actors.

But before the company finally separates the judges have to record their verdicts. They must give a prize in money to the best playwright in tragedy and also in comedy, a prize to the best actor in each, and a prize of a tripod to the well-to-do citizen before-mentioned who had provided and sent in the best-trained and best-equipped chorus. In other words, there is a prize for literature, for acting, and for public spirit. The names of the winners are registered on stone tablets, and the citizen who receives the tripod is generally sufficiently proud of the distinction to present it back to the public, by dedicating it to some temple or placing it on a pedestal in the street known as Tripod Street. One handsome example still remains, though without the tripod, in the shape of the Choragic Monument of Lysicrates.

The only other detail to be mentioned is that, though the theatre belonged to the state, it was farmed out to a lessee, who looked after the building and its repairs, undertook the supply of certain accessories, and therefore charged for admission to all seats but those officially reserved. For the latter there were metal or ivory tickets, tokens or passes, of which some are still in existence, bearing the name of the owner and a number. Except for the reserved places a seat cost two obols — threepence in English silver, but probably equal in value to the modern ninepence. Inasmuch, however, as the festival was religious and the theatre belonged to the public and was under public

R

administration, the state, in the period with which we are dealing, distributed to all citizens who asked for it the said sum of two obols, apparently to do as they chose with. It was their holiday dole from the state, which assumed — not always more rightly than in the experience of modern hospitals — that it would only be the poor who would claim the assistance. There were mean people at Athens, as elsewhere, and Theophrastus tells us of one type in this connection. Towards the end of a performance the lessee did not trouble any longer about the ticket-office, and, says Theophrastus, the mean man would come and bring his boys to the theatre at the hour when the lessee was letting people into the gallery for nothing.

CHAPTER XIII

COUNCIL AND ASSEMBLY

CHAPTER XIII

COUNCIL AND ASSEMBLY

In a previous chapter we dealt with the various classes of the population, namely the citizens, the Outlanders, and the slaves. Among the citizens themselves the great Athenian principle was equality, and that principle was carried to extraordinary lengths. We cannot here go into many details of Athenian administration or of other constitutional antiquities. But in order properly to understand the life of our typical citizen, we must get some fair notion of the part he might be expected to play, besides his military service, in public affairs.

By equality the Athenians did not mean pecuniary equality; they knew the impossibility of that. They meant equal rights and equal opportunities. They had found out the injustices of despotism and oligarchy and class rule, and they endeavoured in every way to guard against undue power of any man or class of men. The possibility of conspiracy or bribery was also always in their minds. Not only was every citizen to be equal before the law; he was to enjoy, as far as human ingenuity could contrive, an equal opportunity of legislating, of holding executive office, and of administering justice. The endeavour was to give, as far as possible, to every one not actually incapacitated his share in these three functions, not in one or other of them. The deliberative Assembly therefore included all respectable citizens; so in actual practice did the law-courts.

It was not, of course, equally feasible for all citizens to be holding executive offices, but every device was tried for distributing those offices as widely as possible. In the first place offices were extremely numerous, and but slenderly paid. The pay was seldom the first consideration, and often it was no consideration at all. Next, besides being numerous, the offices were annual, and there was a provision that no one should hold the same civil office twice. The only exception was membership of the Council of Five Hundred, and twice was the limit even in that instance. In the third place the election to office was by lot. In some functions, it is true, special fitness was indispensable and an election took place accordingly. This was the case with military commanders, the officers of the water-supply, the superintendent of public works, and the occupants of certain high financial posts. The rest were chosen by lot from those who came forward. Black and white beans were put into a vessel and drawn out singly, and the man who drew a white bean received office. There was, however, apparently enough pressure of public opinion to keep the entirely unfit from offering themselves. Moreover, after the lot had been drawn, an officer's personal fitness could be challenged; during his term his performance of his duties could be impeached; his accounts were audited every month; and at the end of his year he was subject to a general inquiry into all his actions. Add that the work in itself was frequently simple routine. The Athenians were also sensitive to public criticism and were eager for public approbation. The system therefore worked better than might have been anticipated. The absolutely incompetent were held back or turned out, and there was secured a fair average of practical ability and experience, which proved very helpful when the same man came to take his part in the deliberations of the Assembly or in the decisions of the law-courts. Beyond this Athens had no "public" or "civil" service. There existed a board of chief magistrates, revenue and treasury officers, temple stewards, police commissioners, a Harbour Board, a Road Board, a Public Buildings Board, a Board for the Market, for the city streets, for weights

FIG. 73. — Athenian weight; public standard.

and measures, for corn supply, for pure food, for the public games, and more besides. But these were simply reputable citizens elected for the year and by lot, and disqualified from serving again. And whatever drawback one may immediately perceive in this system, one may, on the other hand, easily realise that it produced an aggregate of experience which counted for much when the Assembly met to legislate. It was at least better than the American "spoils" system.

But was there no President, no "Ministry" or "Premier"? There were, in one sense at least, none of these things. To whom then would official communications be made by other states, or who would take the initiative in a sudden crisis?

Before answering that question, we must say a word about the "Council" or "Senate." All the power, we have said, lies ultimately with the people. But "the people" as a whole cannot be always together and considering nothing but public business.

FIG. 74. — Athenian coin.

Accordingly a body of 500 citizens of over thirty years of age, chosen annually by lot, formed a sort of standing executive committee of the said people. The members of this body received a drachma (perhaps really worth half-a-crown) a day. They prepared business for the Assembly and attended to matters of urgency. But even 500 are too large a body for daily detail. They were therefore divided again into ten sections of fifty, and each fifty took it in turns to serve as a smaller executive for five weeks. During these weeks the fifty will dine together in a special hall at the public expense; they will give first audience to ambassadors; will be approached first in all matters within the province of the Council; will be conveners of the Council, and will summon meetings of the Assembly, either by fixing up in the Agora those notices which correspond to our government proclamations and advertisements, or else by sending round a trumpeter and crier. Meanwhile one person is chosen by lot every twenty-four hours to be president. He will hold the keys of the treasury and of the archives for just one day and one night. For that time he is practically the head of affairs, but for no longer, nor is he again eligible. If Lysimachus is a councillor, he will thus have 365 chances out of 500 of passing the chair. No legislative proposal can come before the Assembly which the Council has not previously discussed; but nothing which the Council alone decides has any validity. In this large body of 500, annually changed, the Athenians found another means of training thousands of citizens for intelligent public action.

The Assembly, the whole body of full citizens, meets four times in the month, on days advertised by the presiding committee of the Council. It may be also specially summoned by crier and trumpet. Traditionally it meets in the semi-circular space on the hill called the Pnyx, and seats itself as best it can. Nevertheless it might meet elsewhere, and even in the Peiraeus. After the completion of the theatre that building formed a particularly comfortable and convenient place of assembly.

Early in the morning a flag was lifted over the place of meeting, and male citizens of all classes and ages, from twenty upwards, stroll or hasten to the entrances. There they pass before the eyes of watchful scrutineers, specially appointed to see that there is no intruder or disqualified person among them. Each fairly punctual comer receives a token, which he can exchange at the close of the meeting for his fee, the sum of fourpence-halfpenny in Attic money. A sacrifice of purification takes place, and the herald reads a formula of cursing upon all who may speak with treasonable or corrupt motives. Ten persons, with a chairman, are chosen by lot from the members of the Council, and these preside over the meeting. They group themselves on the steps of the platform on the Pnyx, of which we have still the remains. The police-slaves, or "Scythian" archers, are in attendance to keep order. If there is no thunder-storm or earthquake or eclipse or similar phenomenon of bad omen, the business now begins. The herald reads the resolution of the Council, which is to be submitted to the Assembly, or, it may be, the statement of the matter which the Council simply lays before the people. It is illegal for any citizen present to bring up any new business which has not been thus previously discussed by the Council, and a violation of this rule will certainly lead to dangerous prosecution. The citizen will have plenty of opportunity to move either an amendment or the direct opposite of the Council's resolution; but there must be nothing suddenly sprung upon the meeting. The Athenians believed in the sovereignty of the popular will, but not in a popular will hastily and inconsiderately formed. The question is next asked: "Will the Assembly accept the Council's proposal, or shall there be a debate?" A show of hands is taken, and, if a debate is called for, the herald cries, "Who wishes to speak?" In reply, any person present may come forward towards the platform, and, though it is not very clear what would happen if several arrived at once, the position is probably no more awkward than the modern practice of catching the Speaker's eye in Parliament, or the chairman's at a public meeting. Naturally at Athens, as elsewhere, there were a certain number of prominent individuals who were always to the front, and these were known as either "the orators" or "the comers forward." The audience had its favourites, was not gifted with much patience or consideration, and, therefore, in a large measure frightened away the incompetent speaker.

There was, strictly speaking, nothing at Athens corresponding to our party system. The only real cleavages of policy were between the rich and the poor, and were almost entirely financial. The rich, objecting to the drain upon their purses, were inclined to be reactionary, and sometimes attempted oligarchical revolutions; the poor were prone to encourage in their own interests a large public expenditure drawn from the contributions of the wealthy. So far, it is true, there were two parties, or rather two sentiments; but there was no systematic party system or discipline, because there was no such thing as a Ministry, or a threatened dissolution, or any other of those considerations which in modern times bring a party together on every question in defiance of conscientious individual judgment. You would, it is true, have always found in the Athenian Assembly some man of eloquence or force of character who specially voiced the sentiments of the poorer majority. He was known as the "popular champion," and since, in our period, he represented the majority, he was said to "command the stone," that is to say, the platform in the Assembly.

After this digression, let us return to the order of proceedings. A speaker, having mounted the platform, is first of all crowned with a wreath, which at Athens is the outward and visible sign of temporary authority and a claim to security of person. It serves somewhat the purpose of a judge's wig. He is required to speak to the subject, which he may support or oppose or submit to amendment. He requires a clear voice and command of language and gesture, although of the last there must not be too much. The audience is a difficult one to deal with. It yells its disapproval, it bawls for him to come down, it whistles or it applauds with shouts and clapping of hands. If he mispronounces, it mocks him. He must be relevant and interesting, or else he gets no hearing. If he has a proposal or amendment to move, he puts it in writing, and has it clearly read to the assembly. But if he moves anything which is in conflict with some existing law, without waiting for that law to be repealed, he lays himself open to an action for unconstitutional procedure.

When the speaking is over, the president puts the matter to the vote by show of hands. Voting by ballot occurs only in cases which directly affect an individual. If the president sees anything unconstitutional in a proposal, he can refuse to put it, though at his own risk. When carried by the people, the resolution is valid and is recorded in the archives. If it agrees with the opinion of the Council the wording runs, "On the motion of So-and-So it was resolved by the Council and the People." If it differs from the Council's opinion, or if the Council had expressed no opinion, it runs, "It was resolved by the People," and in either case it is equally final.

And here we must stop to say that all this was not "legislation" in the proper sense. It was not passing of *laws*, but only of resolutions affecting foreign policy, a financial measure, or the like. Should there be war? Should so many ships be manned? Should an impeachment be laid against So-and-So?

Nothing is more mistaken than to imagine that sane people

like the Athenians would pass a law, or set of laws, in the Assembly one day and overturn them the next. On the contrary, they most scrupulously watched all resolutions, to see that they contained nothing in violation of existing laws. If you wished a law to be changed, or a new law introduced, you had your suggestion posted up in the Agora side by side with the law already existing. It was then referred to a large court of citizens qualified to be jurymen, who act in this case as a judicial committee of the people. Before this court the old law is arraigned; it is, however, upheld by speakers chosen for the purpose as counsel for the defence; the court gives a decision as to the desirability of a change in the law, and its decision is regarded as the will of the people. All this takes time, and is a most salutary check on hasty or turbulent legislation. When we speak of Athens as exercising a perpetual referendum, we must accept the expression in this sense.

When business is done, the Assembly is dismissed by the presidents, the holders of tickets exchange them for their fee, the flag is hauled down, and the people disperse to their occupations or amusements.

It remains to say that the people were not always particularly eager to attend the Assembly. In some cases the police were sent along the Agora dragging a rope smeared with red chalk, and the citizens were driven before it towards the place of assembly; any one whose clothes were found marked with red was either actually fined or at least denied his fee. Unfortunately we do not know on what occasions, or under what law, this could be done. It was certainly not the usual proceeding, and that is nearly all we can say concerning it.

CHAPTER XIV

AN ATHENIAN TRIAL

CHAPTER XIV

AN ATHENIAN TRIAL

OUR friend Lysimachus can hardly live his life at Athens without experiencing some action at law. Never was there a community more litigious. A character in Aristophanes, to whom a map is being shown, asks which is Attica. When it is pointed out, he refuses to believe, because he cannot "see any lawsuits going on." A man must be engaged in very little public or private business, or must be somewhat lacking in spirit, if he does not at some time appear as either plaintiff or defendant. If he is not suing or being sued in some civil action, he is prosecuting or being prosecuted on some public indictment.

It is very interesting to contemplate an Athenian trial, conducted in a community which possessed no legal profession, no bench of specially trained judges, and no bar of specially trained lawyers. We shall assume that the trial takes place about the middle of our period, and we shall not overburden the account with detail. Lysimachus, let us imagine, brings an action against a certain Isagoras. Very small pecuniary cases are settled by a standing court of forty men, elected by lot for the year; but, where serious interests are involved, the matter is first referred to one of the public arbitrators, a layman, who must be sixty years of age, and his efforts will be to adjust the difficulty. If either party refuses to accept the arbitrator's decision, the case will come before one of those great juries which are among the most striking features of the Athenian democracy. Public and criminal prosecutions will in all cases come before such a jury.

We will suppose that the action of Lysimachus against Isagoras is a public action. Perhaps Isagoras is charged with perjury or with some sort of breach of the peace, which both affects our friend the prosecutor and also the law and order of the state.

Well, Lysimachus, attended by two witnesses, first summons Isagoras to appear before a certain recognised official on a certain day. That official is not the judge, and has nothing to do with trying the case, beyond subsequently introducing it to the court, presiding during the sitting, and seeing that the order of the court is executed. The circumstances are stated before him, and if the official finds the case *prima facie* good, — or a "true bill," — he has the matter prepared for the court. These are his proceedings. He hears no arguing and gives no judgment. The plea is entered and sworn to; its answer is entered and sworn to; witnesses on either side make their statements, which are put in writing, signed, and sworn to. These documents, together with passages cited from the laws, are then sealed up in a special box, called for some reason or other "the hedgehog." A day is appointed for the trial, the order of precedence being determined by lot. The official then takes charge of the box, and no further evidence will be admitted.

Next for the trial proper. At the beginning of the official year a list has been drawn up of about 5000 persons, all of them over thirty years of age, ready to act as jurors for that year. These are divided into ten sections, or panels, of about 500 members each, and each member receives a token or pass marked with the number of his panel. When a case is to be tried, it will be tried by one or other of these panels, but not necessarily in its full strength. There may be 201, or the whole 501, or some other number, presumably determined by the importance of the case. The juryman is not compelled to attend; he is generally only too willing to take part for the sake of the fee or of the business. In very great cases you might have a combination of two full panels with 1001. And be it understood that these men are just plain respectable citizens, and that they are to be both judge and jury, to decide on the law and the facts, and in many instances on the penalty. The theory of Athenian democracy was that judicial decisions belonged, like the deliberative, to the whole people; but in practice it was soon found necessary for the people thus to delegate its powers in this respect to a large jury — a large representative committee of itself, a smaller but faithful copy of itself.

The jurymen have all taken an oath to judge legally and without corruption or bias. Nevertheless there must be a safe-guard against the bribery which was the most rampant public vice of Athens. The manner of preventing the bribing of a jury — if its mere size is not enough — is this. The trial lasts but a day. It is unknown beforehand which panel is to try the case of Lysimachus *versus* Isagoras. On the morning of the trial, the general body of jurymen meets in the Agora, and the jury for a particular case is drawn by lot. Its members proceed to a particular court-house assigned to them, the " Middle Court," or the " Red Court," or the " Hole-and-Corner

Court," or perhaps to the "Hall of Song," or the "Painted Colonnade." Each is provided with a coloured baton of office and his token. On showing these he receives a ticket, which he will give up at the end of the case, receiving in exchange a fee of three obols, or fourpence-halfpenny Attic, for his day's services.

On entering, the jurymen arrange themselves on benches covered with mats; the introducing official presides on a daïs; to the right and left of him are two platforms, from which the parties will speak. The general public are fenced off by a rail, and the public slaves, or police, keep order.

A large water-clock stands in the court and is attended by an officer, who will set it running when bidden and also check the flow when bidden. In most instances, though not in all, the length of time allotted to a speech is limited, or, as it was expressed, the speaking was done "with measured-out day." A sacrifice is made, the "hedgehog" box is unsealed, the clerk reads the accusation and reply, and Lysimachus mounts his platform and pleads. It is absolutely necessary that he should do this in person. If he is himself no speaker, he may have got what was called a "speech-writer" — one of the class of which Demosthenes became the perfection — to compose a speech for him, which he will learn by heart. This, of course, is indirectly employing counsel. Or, after making a brief and unadorned statement, he may, with the consent of the court, be followed by a more eloquent supporter, or perhaps two, although such supporters are theoretically always personal friends assisting gratuitously and from genuine sympathy with his case. In reality they are generally nothing but more expert pleaders. When Lysimachus calls witnesses, it simply means that the signed evidence is taken from the box and read, while the witness himself, when called up, says nothing, but merely signifies that he vouches for what is written. There is no cross-examining, and, it may be as well to add, consequently no badgering. Lysimachus then sits down, and Isagoras rises on his own platform and speaks for himself with or without supporters, and with evidence produced in the same way. Sometimes a second speech is made on each side. This done, a person chosen by lot proceeds to distribute to the jurymen their voting checks. Each juryman receives two checks, one for condemnation and one for acquittal. He is to use which he chooses. In the court stands a large urn, with a narrow mouth, for the reception of the actual vote; at a little distance is a wide-mouthed vessel, into which the other and unused check is to be thrown. Now, as the voting is secret, how can all this be done in open court? The device is ingenious and simple. The voting checks are flat discs of metal, through the middle of which passes a short axle. In one check the axle is hollow — an open pipe; in the other it is solid. The hollow condemns, the solid acquits. The juryman approaches the urn with the ends of the axle held between his fingers, and no one but himself can tell whether it is the solid or the hollow check which he is holding. He drops this into an opening so narrow that he could not drop in two at once if he tried. He then passes to the second vessel and throws in the waste check. When all have paraded, the first urn is turned out upon the stone table, the hollow checks are sorted from the solid, a count is made, and the verdict announced.

We will suppose that the hollow checks are the more numerous, and that Isagoras is condemned. Where there is a statutory penalty this is the end of the trial. But there are cases in which no penalty has been already determined by law. This, let us assume, is one of them. Lysimachus, therefore, when bringing his action against Isagoras, has been obliged to specify the penalty which he thinks ought to be exacted. It may, for example, be a fine, or disfranchisement, or banishment, or death. It will not be imprisonment, for the Athenians only used the prison as a place of detention until a fine was paid or some other sentence was executed. Isagoras being already condemned, it now remains to consider the penalty, and speeches are made by the two sides on this question. Lysimachus proposes the most severe that he thinks the jury will accept; Isagoras proposes the lightest. The jury must necessarily accept the one or the other. When Socrates was on his trial and had been condemned, his opponents proposed death; he himself was inclined to propose that he should receive "free board at the public expense"; but, on the advice of his friends, he ultimately named a fine of £120. It was a common practice for the defendant to bring into court his children or other persons dependent on him, and endeavour to mollify the jury through their tears.

The speeches — shorter in this case — being made, the jury proceeds to vote, either as before or by another device. Instead of checks they may receive one waxed tablet each. A line drawn lengthwise on this means the greater penalty, drawn breadthwise it means the smaller.

After the decision Isagoras is led off by the police-officers and detained in prison until performance of whatever the court has ordered. But, if the penalty were death, he would on a certain day be made to drink a cup of hemlock, of which the effect is to benumb the body gradually, with the minimum of pain or distress, from the feet to the heart. This is the regular form of capital punishment at Athens, except for the lowest criminals. For them it took the barbarous shape of thrashing to death with cudgels.

There perhaps appears not much to commend in the form of an Athenian trial. We are avoiding comment as far as possible, but it may be well to point out one or two considerations. In the first place, Athenian law was comparatively clear and definite, and not beyond the understanding of any intelligent Athenian. In the second, every attempt was made, in civil cases, to get the matter settled by arbitration. In the third, reckless litigation was checked by the knowledge that, if the plaintiff in a private suit lost his case, he paid the expenses, and if he did not obtain one-fifth of the votes, he was fined to boot. In a public prosecution in the same circumstances, he was fined 1000 Attic drachmae, or £40. In the fourth place, every Athenian acquired, by habitual attendance at the court and in the Assembly, such a ready grasp of points as one would hardly find in a modern jury, but would rather look for in a professional lawyer. No doubt there were appeals to passion, but hardly more so than in addresses to a modern jury. On the whole, we may doubt whether the verdict of a casual modern twelve is much better than the verdict of a casual Athenian five hundred. The real evil was rather that the existence of the system bred an army of blackmailers, who were always spying upon wealthy or prominent persons and threatening to bring some action, or at least trouble their peace, unless they were bought off.

CHAPTER XV

BURIAL

CHAPTER XV

BURIAL

THE latest and worst misfortune that could befall a human being was to be left an unburied and unhonoured corpse. Charon would not receive you into his boat, and your poor ghost was left to shiver, helpless and miserable, between the confines of the two worlds. To be buried without honour and to occupy a neglected tomb meant that your wretched ghost became a pariah among the departed. A first duty of the relatives was therefore to pay to the deceased what were known as the "dues" or "rights." In the first place the eyelids were carefully closed, the body was washed and anointed with perfumes, fillets and a garland of flowers were wreathed round the head, and usually a silver or copper coin was placed in the mouth. And here for a moment we must digress. We must carry ourselves back from our cultured Athenian days to a stage of human development in which it is imagined that the departed are simply making a journey to another world, in which they will require the same things which they required in this life — food, clothing, money, armour, vessels, and the like, and, in the case of children, dolls and playthings. In the case of women an indispensable article was a mirror. At that early stage it was well understood why such articles were buried with the body. But, as we all know, in matters of custom and sentiment practices are long kept up when their meaning is lost, and when fanciful reasons are wont to be invented in place of true reasons forgotten.

The coin placed in the mouth of the departed was commonly explained as intended to pay the fee due to Charon for ferrying the ghost over the river Styx. Originally it was simply a provision of money. But why put it in the mouth? Because, unsavoury proceeding as it may appear, a common way of holding small change in antiquity was to pouch it in your cheeks, somewhat after the style of monkeys. Any day in the Athenian market it would be possible to see one of the poorer classes, on receiving small coins, pop these into his mouth, until he could more conveniently dispose of them. So much for "Charon's obol."

The body is now clothed in fine white raiment, and laid upon a couch spread with rich clothes and scattered with marjoram. The feet are turned towards the door. Close by are tables, upon which are placed the slender and graceful vessels which must always go into the grave, and also such other things as are thought fit, including a honey-cake, which was popularly regarded as a sop to be given to Cerberus, the three-headed watch-dog of Hades. Around are the kinsfolk, lamenting according to a conventional and orthodox method, whether with deep earnestness or without. This lying-in-state was of course meant for honour to the corpse, but there is little doubt that it was also once intended as an assurance to all concerned that the man was really dead, and that he had died without foul play.

History does but repeat itself when in modern times we send wreaths to a funeral. This was regularly done by friends and relatives at Athens. It is recorded of a certain professional beauty, to whom one of her suitors kept sending flowers instead of the more substantial presents which she expected, that she reminded him she was "not yet a corpse untimely dead."

If, passing along the Athenian streets, you were to see an earthenware vessel containing water placed outside a door, you might conclude that there was a lying-in-state within, and, if you waited, you would see each friend or kinsman, as he came out, sprinkle himself therefrom. This action, partly sanitary, has become purely symbolic.

On the following day, before sun-up, comes what was called the "carrying-out," or funeral procession. The body, still lying on the couch, is carried through the streets, either in a vehicle or on the shoulders of friends or slaves, to a place outside the walls. Just in front will march the male mourners, and the female mourners just behind. These have cut their hair short and are dressed in black. If the defunct was a person of means, his destination will probably be the road which runs through the suburb Cerameicus, or else some other equally frequented. If poor or a slave, he must be buried in the necropolis, outside the gate as you go to the harbour-town of Peiraeus. With the body will be carried the tables full of vases and other articles. In front, or behind, will walk professional dirge-singers, principally women from Asia Minor hired for the purpose. These not only chant as they walk to the accompaniment of a flute, but also go through symbolical performances of rending the garments, beating the breast, and tearing the hair and cheeks. In early days such extravagant demonstrations were expected in real earnest of the real mourners, relatives, and slaves, but at our date these were expressly forbidden by law to Athenian citizens.

When the procession reaches its destination, the body is either buried or cremated. The two methods went on side by side, but cremation was the more expensive, and, therefore, naturally the less frequent. If you were cremated, the bones and ashes — which are easily distinguishable from those of the fuel — were gathered together by the nearest relatives, washed in wine, and placed in a vessel of bronze or earthenware, which again was placed in the family tomb. If you were buried, a coffin was usual, though not necessary, and this might be made of wood, but was more commonly of earthenware. To have " one foot in the coffin " is a Greek proverb which we have borrowed. On the funeral pyre, or into the grave, are generally thrown vessels, ornaments, sometimes garments, and other expensive gifts. It was a point of sentiment to burn or bury with the body anything which had been specially affected in life.

It now remains for the procession to return home to a ceremonial meal, at which the chief feature will be a series of eulogies of the dead man and his virtues. The resemblance between this proceeding and an Irish wake, despite all the differences of taste, is too obvious to miss. The explanation is that the ceremonies were of common origin.

Meanwhile it is worth while to glance at the nature of the tombs or monuments which lined the road to the Academy or some other egress from Athens. These were mostly in excellent taste. They were by no means all alike. On an elevation made of earth and stones were sometimes erected upright slabs of stone, chiefly with gable tops and with reliefs carved on their fronts ; sometimes round pillars with ornamental heads surmounted a number of steps; sometimes actual buildings shaped like small temples were built with columns and roofs. The reliefs which such monuments bear have nothing vulgarly sentimental about them. Artistically they are often admirable, though in many cases they are the comparatively crude work of the monumental mason. By preference they represented the character or pursuits of the deceased by means of typical scenes in his life. The young cavalryman is seen on horseback

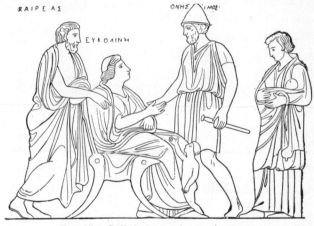

Fig. 75. — Relief on a tomb: parting scene.

striking down the enemy; the kindly parent is seen with his children at a family meal; the workman is seen at his work; the endeared old nurse is receiving the parting handshake of her former nurselings. A water-pot on the tomb of a girl was taken to mean "died unmarried."

Inscriptions are few and brief. Usually the name of the deceased and of his father — that is to say, his official name — sufficed. There was no epitaph setting forth his virtues, except that sometimes there was added the single Greek word which means "a good man" or "a good woman" as the case might be. At a later date, or in other parts of Greece, or among foreigners at Athens, there were, it is true, longer inscriptions, regularly written in a special form of epigrammatic verse; but

FIG. 76. — Ceremony at tomb.

they were altogether the exception in the case of the classical Athenian proper. Theophrastus observes, in satire of the character called the "Officious Man," that he "will inscribe upon a deceased woman's tombstone the name of her husband, of her father, of her mother, as well as her own, with the place of her birth; recording further that 'all these were estimable persons.'"

If we follow the bereaved family home, we shall find that they regard it as a duty to carry offerings and decorations to the tomb, and to perform certain domestic ceremonies on at least the third, the ninth, and the thirtieth day after the death, and also on the birthday of the deceased. An illustration of such pious performance may here be shown; it is notable that in it the dead person is represented as if present. To neglect the tomb of your ancestors was so far a crime that no man could become a chief officer of the state who could be proved to have failed in this respect. And, lastly, when the Greeks in Aeschylus cheer each other on to fight with the overwhelming numbers of the Persians, one chief incentive is to "set free the tombs of the forefathers."

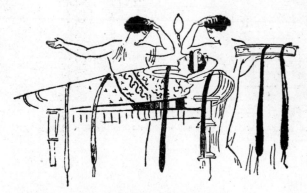

FIG. 77. — Laying out the dead.

CHAPTER XVI

ATHENIAN ART

CHAPTER XVI

ATHENIAN ART

An adequate account of Athenian art would involve the treatment of Athenian music, painting, sculpture in its various branches, and architecture. It would involve also the mention of many dates and persons, accompanied with a long list of technical terms.

But our purpose is not to accumulate a set of undigested, and perhaps indigestible, facts and speculations, but to bring home as distinctly as possible the special quality and character of Attic art. If we speak of Attic fine art, we must not waste time with vague rhetoric and rhapsodies of admiration. There is nothing about which it is so easy to talk for hours, and yet say nothing definite and understandable after all, as "art." And perhaps there is nothing about which it is more difficult to communicate to other minds exactly what one sees and feels, than this same "art."

We may limit our treatment of the subject almost entirely to that branch of Attic art which was most characteristic and most perfect — the art of sculpture — the art in which no modern has ever equalled Pheidias, Praxiteles, or Lysippus. The forceful Michael Angelo on the one hand, the smooth Canova on the other, have perhaps in their best examples rivalled the Greeks of the decline. Nevertheless, the pre-eminence of Pheidias and Praxiteles remains unassailed, and seems likely to remain so for ever.

As regards architecture, it is a commonplace to tell how pure in conception and sometimes how magnificent in impressiveness was a building like the Parthenon on the hill-top of Athens. But this classical style of building is imitable, and was freely and not unsuccessfully imitated, perhaps even successfully modified, in many parts of the Graeco-Roman world; it could, perhaps, be reproduced tolerably to-day; while that which really distinguished the Parthenon as the queen of edifices was rather its sculptures on frieze and pediment than its merely architectural style. Nor is Attic architecture, though unsurpassable in its own kind, necessarily the consummation of the art of building. The Gothic of Cologne Cathedral and Giotto's tower at Florence are, we may surely admit, as high in the scale of artistic conception and performance.

We may, therefore, make but a passing reference here to architecture, although it is well to point out how, like other arts, it conformed in principle to the invariable Greek demand for perfection of a noble simplicity.

On Greek painting we need but make a note. The names of Polygnotus and Zeuxis are to us but names. We are not, it is true, without such literary description of their works as to show that a Polygnotus was capable of large and complicated designs in fresco, such as he created on the " Painted Porch " of Athens and in the loggia at Delphi; that he was a brilliant colourist; and that he could paint not merely the body but in some degree the soul that informed it. We are told in the old story that Zeuxis and Parrhasios could paint so realistically as to deceive the birds and each other. Zeuxis painted his grapes so that they attracted the birds, and Parrhasios painted a curtain so that Zeuxis tried to draw it aside. We may believe these stories as little as we like, remembering the Greek, if not the universal, tendency to polish up the marvellous into its most telling form. Next we hear in the technical books of Graeco-Roman times a good deal about the management of light and shade, and about the mixing and manipulating of colours, and so forth; and everything goes to show that the Greek artists could draw admirably, produce splendid colour-effects, and design artistic conceptions. And yet we may certainly believe that in the deeper virtues of painting they were not the equals of the great Italian and Spanish masters, and that our best modern artists could teach them much which they would have been only too glad, and exceedingly swift, to learn.

As it happens, all these Greek paintings of the higher kind have naturally disappeared. We cannot expect to meet with masterpieces more than two thousand years old. All we possess are rather insignificant frescoes of Graeco-Etruscan or Graeco-Roman work, unearthed from Pompeii or elsewhere, and paintings on vases, which are often either not pure Greek or do not represent the higher efforts of masters.

Of Greek music we know but little. The Greek ear was exceedingly well-trained, exceedingly acute, in matters of time and pitch; and the system of keys was something exceedingly elaborate; but they knew nothing of harmony, and we should not, at this date, regard them as even tolerable musicians.

Athenian music has vanished, Athenian painting of the classical time has also vanished, Athenian architecture can be imitated, as well as equalled in another kind. But the Greek carving of stone or casting of bronze into statues, Greek gem-engraving and coin-engraving, Greek shapes in pottery and metal-ware; these stand alone in the world for an entire and characteristic perfection.

And, therefore, our few and salient types of Athenian art in illustration of salient principle will be best taken from sculpture. We cannot here range far nor probe deep; our task is to be as definite as it is possible to be when speaking succinctly of matters so evasive of expression as aesthetic principles.

The aim of all Greek art, in the day of its perfection, was to express with a noble simplicity and truth something intrinsically worthy of expression. That principle was cardinal, and it must be held always in view. But there was in each art a period of infancy, a period of development, one of full bloom and maturity, and one of decay. This too should be borne in mind, inasmuch as nearly all the confusion which exists in the popular conception as to the qualities and characteristics of Greek literature or Greek sculpture or Greek vase-painting is due to a confounding of dates and styles. A miscellaneous collection of Greek sculptures, without classification according to chronology, would leave the observer hopelessly perplexed. He has perchance been told that Greek sculpture is especially characterised by beauty of form, and then, when he comes to discover many an ugliness or stiffness in the examples before him, he will wonder how such a doctrine can be tenable. But, if we were to eliminate the crude apprentice-work whereby the earlier Greeks sought honestly but ineffectually to body forth their Apollos and Athenas and other deities; if we were to label these efforts as archaic and immature; if, in other words, we were to warn the observer that these are not true specimens of Greek art, but only efforts towards Greek art; then we might bring him to see how, in nearly all that remained, beauty of form was indeed a constant element.

Or, again, he has been told that Greek sculpture is typical rather than individual, and yet, when he comes to contemplate the mixed assemblage of Greek creations in marble or bronze, he may discover works which are obviously copies from some strongly marked individual sitter, or some strikingly individual pose, and, before he can understand this contradiction, he must needs be told that Greek art, like every other, had its period of decadence, which was not its Greek but its "Hellenistic" and "Graeco-Roman" period, and that, in this period, the true Greek principle is dying out of recognition.

We are therefore to bear in mind that the term "Athenian art," if unqualified, means Athenian art when it was both most characteristic and most perfect; that is to say, in the great age which began in the middle of the fifth century B.C. and lasted for a hundred and fifty years.

With this understanding we may repeat our text, that the aim of Greek art was to express with a noble simplicity and truth something intrinsically worthy of expression. And first the thing must be worthy of expression. All genuine Athenian art was democratic. Take sculpture again, for example. It was not, in the best days, addressed to the whim of a single person or to the taste of an illuminate coterie. The artist appealed to the great world and to the general heart and eye of humanity. But the world at large is not seeking primarily to know how skilful an artist may be in the representation of this and that thing which simply happens to be difficult to represent. Professional artists may be disproportionally interested in such questions; it is natural that they should be.

But the Athenian community, for whom the contemporary artist worked, asked simply for a creation upon which it could on all days and in all generations look with pleasure or admiration or reverence. Say what one will of the public of that democracy, it at least showed no taste for trivialities, when it came to building its temples and adorning its shrines and its public places. The gods, the exploits of gods and men, the figures of men and women serving as striking types of health and beauty, these, together with such action as conduced to the display of dignity, majesty, beauty, and health, were subjects of sculpture. Noble deaths too have their place. But there is no place for the representation, however dexterous, however consummate, of things lewd and prurient, of the vile and ugly, of human indignity and vulgarity. If you had told the Athenians — as you would have had a perfect right to do — that art means representation, they would not have denied it. If you had said that therefore art was just as much art whether it bodied forth the noble or the mean, the sublime or the ludicrous, they might have admitted it. But they would have said that, inasmuch as the choice lay with the artist to represent either the one or the other, it was wasteful folly for him to spend on the execution of the trivial or the repulsive the gift which he might have been spending on the noble or beautiful. At any rate — and yet they were no Puritans, but just sane and wholesome pagans with clear heads and true tastes — they would, as a public of patrons and spectators, have nothing to say to these exhibitions of skill in mistaken directions. Throughout all the truly classical period you will find nothing embodied by Athenian artists in stone or in metal which does not either carry with it some feeling of majesty and dignity, heroism or

other loftiness, or else stir the mind to keen pleasure in the
contemplation of physical and mental perfection — the perfection of strength, grace, or beauty. Not that the Athenians
deliberately meant their art to preach to men. Their choice
of these higher and healthier themes was intuitive or inbred,
the spontaneous outcome of a judgment sane and true.

We do not, of course, worship the Athenian gods, nor do
we worship the human body as did the Athenians: our
sympathies are as limited on the one side as the Athenian
sympathies were on another. To us, therefore, an Athenian
sculpture, even of the best period, may sometimes seem to lack
motive. But that is our misapprehension, and, even while we
are making it, we can scarcely fail to see that the form is
perfect and the execution absolutely true.

That is the next point — the Athenian resolve to be true in
execution, true with a fine and noble simplicity ; to be true to
the exact degree to which truth is desirable, and to stop there ;
not to stop earlier, nor yet to pass beyond into such a finical
and distracting elaboration of detail as to take from the intended effect of the whole. Many people imagine that Greek
sculpture — to take that salient province again — deliberately
avoided truth to nature, and aimed at some utterly conventional
thing called "the ideal." Nothing could be more mistaken.
The whole aim of Greek sculpture was to reproduce the living
man or woman, and the sublime of its execution was attained
only when the carving seemed to be instinct with life, a life
not merely of the limbs, but a life of the soul, which informed
the countenance and was felt to be controlling every limb. A
Greek sculptor like Praxiteles studies long and lovingly every
action of the human muscles and every proportion of the best-

built bodies in every worthy pose or exercise, as they showed themselves in the wrestling-grounds or in his workshop. He studies the human countenance in all worthy moods. To anatomy he is as true as artist need wish to be. But are not his figures "ideal"? Doubtless, but what does "ideal" mean? That they are abstract, conventional, or frankly superhuman? Anything but that. It means simply that he carves figures which, while entirely true to strict anatomy, entirely lifelike in all their delicate modelling and in their strong yet graceful suppleness, are examples of nature in happiest circumstance, of that which nature evidently means perfect man to be, of that which is quite conceivably attainable by man, and is now and then actually attained by him — rather this, than mere vigorous or skilful copies of surrounding men and women, with various physical shortcomings upon them.

That is the sort of "truth to nature" which the Greeks thought fit to set up for delight and admiration in their temples and colonnades.

There is finally the element of a fine and noble simplicity. In all the best of Athenian art the effects are utterly truthful and satisfying. But how is this truth obtained? Perhaps scarcely otherwise than by sheer genius, combining the most luminous observation with a perfect technical mastery over the material. Return to sculpture once again. How are we to embody a deity, in form the ideal man or woman, ideal in strength and grace and that perfection of spirited character which the Athenians call ἀρετή, revealing in the countenance a certain "divine energy of contemplation"? By what means, in representing such a divinity, shall the sculptor impart to the stone or the bronze these physical and spiritual perfections?

FIG. 78. — Hermes of Praxiteles.

How shall he realize the light grace of movement in an Aphrodite, or her look of melting but divine charm ? How the quiet benignity of a Hermes holding the infant Bacchus ? There is

Fig. 79. — Laocoon.

no scope here for all the pronounced, and in a sense loud, anatomical chisel-play of him who sculptures the writhing group of the Laocoon or the gigantic muscles of the Farnese

Hercules. The artist must rely simply on a perfect modelling, into which can come no tricks and *tours de force*. For just the perfect smile, the eyelid and the lips and the moulding of the cheek must receive treatment so infinitely delicate, that none can say exactly how it is accomplished. The chisel of Praxiteles seems to have been inspired by Nature personified.

Such is the fine and noble simplicity which the perfect age of Greek art preferred to all the cleverest anatomical studies in contorted limbs and starting veins and faces drawn with agony or puckered with glee. There is nothing conventional here, nothing easy and imitable, rather the consummately difficult and the inimitable, because so utterly final in its veracity. The Athenian public, keenly observant of the human body and countenance, were merciless judges of the veracious and the lifelike in matters so hard to seize. The artist was therefore practically driven to perfection.

Though, then, the Athenians did not ask art to preach, and probably never thought out just what they did ask of it, they required that it should deal with things not mean nor trivial nor ugly ; that it should not slavishly copy accidental and peculiar facts of individual occurrences, but should seek that type which is the aim of nature's effort, the ideal. Though they demanded of it simplicity, simplicity meant anything rather than want of skill and finish ; it meant that very perfection of performance which renounces every trick, and rests for its effects solely upon absolute truth.

The same fine simplicity appears in Greek architecture and in Greek literature. Aristotle says of the best literary style that it should be "clear but not undistinguished." So Greek architecture is building, "but not undistinguished." It is when we begin to add the distinction that we run the risk of errors in taste. It is a prime excellence of Greek art that its taste was right in the matter of "distinguishing" its writing

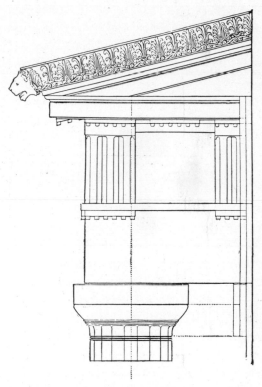

FIG. 80. — Doric style.

or its building. Imagine a row of stately columns before some noble structure; let those columns be Doric, Ionic, Corinthian, as you will. It will be noticed that their shafts are all simple, and that such ornament as they possess is at the capital, where

u

the horizontal and vertical lines are to meet. The ornament is there for a purpose, to spare the abruptness of transition from

FIG. 81. — Ionic style.

the one line to the other. The expansion in the capital of an Ionic or Corinthian column seems to gather up the weight of

the superincumbent mass, and which shape the ornament shall
take is fairly a " matter of taste," though it may be remarked
that the more florid Corinthian is rather affected in Graeco-
Roman than in classical Athenian times.   Now, again, suppose
we begin to modify those shafts by means of grooves or flutings

running vertically.   Here the
eye is not displeased.   There
is not merely a relieving of the
monotony, but there is significance in the fact that those
lines or grooves running up the
column seem by an illusion to
help in the supporting strength
and natural upward striving of
the pillars.   So far goes the
Greek.   But go further than
that, and begin to bedeck the
same shafts at intervals with
festoonings and reliefs and fantastic figurings of fruits and
flowers and heads of cherubs
and animals and so forth, and
good taste at once revolts.   The
ornamentation is meaningless,
it helps nothing, it is obtrusive ;

FIG. 82. — Corinthian style.

it cries out, " I am merely intended for a prettiness," and it
offends.   It is much the same with literature, and in writing,
as in architecture, modern taste is less true than the Greek.
Very many, perhaps the greater number, feel no offence at the
filigree-work on the columns.   Indeed it by no means rarely

happens that it is precisely these ornaments of which many are most enamoured.

When it is asked why the Greeks, and particularly the Athenians, were so pre-eminently artistic a people, why their fine art was so plenteous and so admirable, the usual answer is insufficient. To say that their peculiar love of art and their peculiar mastery of its principles came of a special "genius" in the race, is only partially true. No doubt, as a people, the Greeks actually were distinguished by a superlative dexterity of hand and a rare truth of taste. From their happy racial blending it seems to have resulted that the Hellenes in the main stood to most other peoples somewhat as the individual of higher tastes and perception among ourselves may stand to the individual of lower taste and insight. That they loved and honoured art is clear from Fig. 83, in which is depicted the interior of a pottery with Athena and two Victories present to reward the workers, one of whom is a woman. But we must not make too much of national genius, a thing which in some cases is almost as much an effect as a cause. No doubt the Greek is always so far superior to the Roman or the Oriental in the principles and practices of his literature, his sculpture, and his architecture alike, that we must assuredly give him credit for a type of mind congenitally higher than theirs in these aesthetic domains. And yet this type of mind was itself in no inconsiderable degree developed or encouraged by special circumstances, and we can hardly tell how far the same circumstances, had they existed, might have produced a nobler and purer type of artistic creation in Egypt or in Rome. For take an example. It was the new circumstances of the

Fig. 83. — Scene of vase-painters.

later Italian cities which called forth the wealth of painting, sculpture, architecture, and literature which belongs to Renaissance times. The people themselves were the same. Similarly it was what we may call a long-sustained local rivalry of devotion, that called forth the Gothic cathedrals which cover North-Western Europe.

And what was the case with Greece? Greece in all probability borrowed its first principles of architecture or sculpture from the Egyptians and the Asiatics. Its literature it devised for itself, and therefore its literature, unlike its early sculpture, was in the Greek style from the first. But the rudimentary efforts of Greek architectural and plastic art are evidently imitative. Their Egyptian or Oriental character can escape no observer, even if he be but moderately informed. It is often difficult at the first glance to distinguish the early Greek work from that of Egypt. Now the Egyptian artists in stone or wood were craftsmen of marvellous dexterity. They seem to have done what they liked with the material. When the fully formed and settled Greeks first came into intercourse with Egypt, they knew nothing of the sculptor's and very little of the builder's art, whatever may have been the artistic potentialities with which nature had endowed them as a race. They found themselves face to face with people who could take stone and shape it deftly into separate figures of gods and men, or into pillars with ornate capitals, or carve it into whole scenes in relief along a temple or palace front. What more natural than that they, the Greeks, should set themselves to do the same? Would it have been surprising if their art had continued to cultivate just the forms and follow just the conventions of those who first taught them how to create a shape and handle a chisel ?   The Egyptian hand was as sure as the Greek.   In the Egyptian Museum of Boulac there are specimens of perfectly realistic portraiture in wood or stone, which could hardly be surpassed for mere technical skill.   This being so, since Greek art began by copying the Egyptian, and since the best Egyptian workman was as dexterous as the Greek, how comes it that the art of Greece took so different a course, produced work so characteristically its own, so immeasurably higher in all the effects of beauty and noble interest ?

Because, it is said, of the superiority of Greek genius in the region of taste.   That natural superiority cannot be denied; but we are bound to point out that there were other reasons. Three are patent.   Greek social organisation, Greek religious ideas, and Greek physical training had quite as much to do with the matter.   We may, if we choose, call these also part of the peculiar Greek genius, and so we come back to the Greek genius after all.   But then it is not solely the spontaneous aesthetic genius of the Greeks which decides the question of Greek art.   It is that congenital aesthetic genius finding free play in a peculiar social organisation and a peculiar range of religious and social ideas, although these are themselves but another outcome of the Greek genius in the intellectual and social domains.

Let us endeavour to make this clear.   In Egypt we find an absolute monarchy tempered by priestly power, a caste-system, a worship of mysterious and monstrous deities, and a remarkable belief in the possibility of prolonging a desirable existence for the dead, either by mummifying the corpse or by providing it with a " double " in the shape of an image.   At what then will

Egyptian art be aiming? Necessarily it will build dark and mysterious shrines; it will carve monsters to represent its gods, monsters which are neither ideal nor real; it will build kings' palaces, and carve and paint scenes full of their victories, scenes in which the king is everything, while the individual who does the fighting counts for nothing and need only be conventionally depicted. In Egypt, therefore, we shall find no ideal types of sculpture, no aiming at the representation of perfect strength and beauty.

But how is it with Greece? In the first place the Greek gods are simply glorified humanity possessed of more perfect powers of mind and shapes of body. There is no symbolism about them. And Greek art began with Greek religion. The first objects to be carved were therefore gods; and here at once Greek sculpture must break away from the Egyptian, with its dog-headed and cow-headed monstrosities, or from the Assyrian, with its winged bulls and griffin-beaked demons. It must seek to represent real and true forms, though more perfect than the common reality.

Remember that Greece consisted of a multitude of little states and cities, each with local tutelary deities of its own, and with a local pride and ambition of its own. The consequence was that hundreds upon hundreds of temples of special divinities, adorned with their statues within and without, rose all over Greece. Hence an increasing competition in the production of these human but ideal forms, and therefore a continual improvement in technical methods, a continual approach towards the desired perfection. In Egypt there were a few national gods and these were carved practically alike all over the kingdom. In Greece each little state demanded a realisation of its own conception of its special deity or set of deities, and was eager to surpass its neighbours in the excellence of the result. It was not simply taste for true art, though that counted for much. It was partly also real devotion to the deity, partly the same rivalry which at a later time in Italy induced Venice, Florence, or Genoa to beautify themselves one against the other. Nothing could foster great sculpture better than this — first, a deliberate aim at the representation of ideal humanity, second, a constant stimulus of rivalry on all sides towards its perfect attainment.

In the third place the Greek states in which art most flourished were democracies. There was abundance of popular criticism proceeding from an intelligent people, who, after all, recognise truth to the human form when they see it. The appeal was not to academies or cliques, to a patron or to a priesthood. It was to the truth of nature. And this fact, so long as Greek states were democratic, kept art fresh and wholesome and natural. The fantastic, the exaggerated, the finical, the untrue, belong, and always have belonged, to passing schools and coteries, or to hidebound sects. In all the best periods of art it has been the artist who executes and the aggregate of laymen who judge. It is only in decadent periods that the artist judges himself or is judged by his own particular school. Pheidias built and carved, Praxiteles sculptured, in order to perform to his best ability what the community sought from him.

And in the last place, besides the rivalry, the aim at the ideal of true humanity, and the lively intelligent popular appreciation, there existed, for sculpture, the all-important fact that the Greeks knew, as no other civilised nation has ever known, what the human body is like. For hundreds of years

the Greeks wrestled and leapt and ran and threw the quoit
and the javelin in their training-schools and public games in
a state of nudity. We in modern times may be students of
anatomy and know the body theoretically. The sculptor or
painter may share in that study, so far as often to carve and paint
rather anatomy than life. The Greek artists and the Greek
critics of artists knew the body simply as it was; they could
study it every day in every pose and every outline. And,
since the purpose of art is to express to the life what you see,
because you see it, and not to express some underlying fact
which you may have been taught by science, the Greeks carved
their statues true to ideal life, representing in absolute perfection
that which was lifelike from a spectator's point of view. What
more can possibly be desired? The Greek artist did not say,
"I shall shape this thus and thus because science tells me that
it ought to be so." He simply said, "This is the shape we look
for in the finest types in the gymnasia."

Such are the religious and social conditions which helped
to make Greek art follow a line so different from the Oriental.
They apply to buildings and to paintings as much as they do
to statuary. Nevertheless, do not let us be understood to
deny that, naturally and congenitally, the Greek taste and
spirit sought the true expression, with a fine and noble
simplicity, of something worthy to be expressed. For it is so
in Greek literature also, as far back as we can go, as far back
as our Homer, and, we may be wholly certain, beyond our
Homer.

These then are the reasons — true aims and true criticism —
why Greek art reached so high a standard. And why was it

so plenteous ? We at this day can hardly realise how full Greece must have been of noble building and noble sculpture. Ancient writers, like Pausanias, describe to us immense numbers of statues. For centuries these people were building their temples and public edifices, and erecting masterpieces of sculpture in them. Many a town or its acropolis must have been a perfect museum of art works. Statues on the level ground, statues on high pedestals, statues seated in the shrines, statues placed in the pediments, sculptures in relief along the frieze, on altars, and on tombs — temples lifting their bright columns and coloured gables on countless hills and promontories against the background of the blue sky or the mountains — paintings in the colonnades and lounging-places — how little of all this is left!

The Romans ransacked Greece and carried off innumerable masterpieces to Italy, where, after the barbarian invasions, the marble figures were mostly burnt for lime and the bronze figures melted down for the metal, while only a few, and those not of quite the best period, have managed to escape. The emperors of Constantinople carried off large numbers of the remainder, only to let them fall later into the iconoclastic hands of the Turks. The Slav and Frank and Venetian and Turk have played their parts in the havoc. Time and neglect have done the rest. And so it comes about that, whereas we possess such treasures as the Elgin marbles from the Parthenon and the "Aeginetan marbles" from Aegina, the Hermes of Praxiteles unearthed in 1877 at Olympia, reliefs from the altars of Pergamus and from the Mausoleum, and rather late works like the Laocoon and the Aphrodite of Melos, for the most part we possess no original work direct from the hand of a great master. Beautiful, and in some cases fully authenticated, copies of the great masterpieces, dating from the later Greek or Graeco-Roman times, are to be found in museums like the Vatican or that of Naples. Enough material has been found to overthrow almost entirely the doctrines of Greek art formulated on such slight material by critics of the last century. But, after all, it is but a poor fraction of all this Greek work that we either now possess or can ever hope to possess when the last excavator has dug his last shovelful.

The plenteousness of excellent work at Athens came partly from the inbred popular love of art, which constantly demanded such creations; partly from the fact that the typical Athenian was mainly a man of leisure and yet of energy, whose activities must find effusion in some direction, and therefore found it largely in art; and partly from the fact that the Athenians were a people of simple lives, of no domestic extravagance, caring rather more for the things of the mind than those of the body, and therefore prepared to devote their funds liberally to the beautifying of their city and the gladdening of their own eyes. Art, in fact, was a fashion as well as a passion. It was a part of their life, not an element of esoteric cultivation.

The effect of Athenian life on Athenian art is, then, sufficiently clear. It is less easy to demonstrate the influence of Athenian art on Athenian life. Yet such an influence was undoubtedly exerted. For instance, take religion. The Greek gods were from the first held to be like unto men, though in the better minds they were superior to men, possessing all the highest of human attributes. Yet if the ordinary Greek had been left to the tales of the current mythology for his conception of divinity, his deities would have been but gross, and rather to be feared than held in willing reverence. Art

Fig. 84. — Bust of Pericles.

played an altogether unique part in raising the standard of deity, that is to say, in refining and ennobling the conception

of it.   Artist vying with artist to represent ideally in visible
form the omnipotent majesty of Zeus, or the calm benignant
wisdom of Athena, or the chaste maidenhood of Artemis —
artist vying with artist to set these and other gods in temples
more and more worthy to be the abodes of awe and majesty;
these, working through the eyes and upon the sentiments of
men, undoubtedly raised up better notions of the godhead,
and to an appreciable extent modified Athenian religion, at
least on its theoretical side.   Athena as conceived by the
Athenians was the Athena as carved by Pheidias, and, however
imaginary a being Athena may have been, it was manifestly
better that the patron goddess should be imagined in such
perfection than according to an individual fancy, which might
be, and in many cases was sure to be, vulgar and uninspiring.

It is to the sculptor's and painter's art that is due the
characteristic quality of Greek deities, as conceived from the
great age of Greek life onward — the quality which the Greeks
themselves called σεμνότης, a difficult word to translate, but im-
plying a character which must impress and chasten with its
superior excellence and dignity.   Doubtless the sculptor and the
painter had first to entertain the general Greek notion that gods
are glorified men and women; but it was they who determined,
or by rivalry developed, the ideal of that glorifiying or σεμνότης.

To raise the standard of your gods is to raise the standard
of your conception of your relation to those gods, and thus art
produced some practical effect upon the spiritual life of Athens,
in so far — and it was not very far — as the spiritual life was
determined by religion.

Meanwhile, on the social side, the effect of such a wealth of
fine conceptions, forms of health and grace and beauty and

dignity, seen every day, set a perpetual standard for physical development, for personal bearing and demeanour, which had

FIG. 85. — Bust of Plato.

its influence upon the individual. "Beautiful as a statue" was a current phrase, and perhaps it was a more wholesome thing for a Greek to form himself generation after generation

upon the ideals of artists, than to vary, as we do, according
to that highly capricious and often stultifying thing called
"fashion." Greek art was very clear in its principles and
very consistent in its practice, and though it might be difficult,
amid the modern turbid or anarchic conditions of art and the
slight popular regard for it, to imagine art operating practically
upon our behaviour, the case with Greek art and its art-loving
people must be judged from quite another standpoint.

There is still to be mentioned one fact which is apt to give
a shock to the modern student of aesthetics. This was the
painting or tinting of statuary. As we look at the Elgin
marbles or the Hermes of Praxiteles, figures so perfect in
modelling and of such fine texture of the marble, we find it
difficult to believe that the artist deliberately coloured the hair
or eyes or painted portions of the drapery. Yet such is the
truth. The marks of the paint and even portions of it are still
discernible. But it would leave an altogether false impression
upon our minds if we left the statement in that bald shape.

The modern is puzzled and vexed, and perhaps not un-
naturally. Egyptian and Assyrian sculpture and building were
invariably coloured. The object originally was to render the
thing represented more lifelike, as well as to bring out the
figures and shapes with more distinctness. The outlines stood
out better against the sky or other background; but mainly
the purpose was to recall the actual thing, to be realistic in
colour as in shape. When the Greeks, in their artistic infancy,
learned their lessons from the Egyptians and others, they
learned also to colour the first rough images of gods which
they made. The poor things needed it; they were such un-
lifelike creations. They were mostly of wood, with legs and

x

arms not separated, made like dolls, with eyes of glass or more precious material let in, and with real hair inserted into the scalp. And therewith they were coloured from head to foot, with such skill as the artificer could command. Then, in their rapid progress—for it was marvellously rapid—the shapes improved, the limbs separated, the hair was carved instead of inserted, and the colour began to be more sparingly and artistically employed. Yet it was found that, when contemplated from a distance, as these crudely fashioned deities mostly were, the colour gave distinctness to what might have been otherwise hardly discernible. Moreover, as no one had yet seen sculpture without colour, so no one yet thought of sculpture without colour. The artist and his employers, the public, both stood in need of experience.

But one thing the artist began instinctively to do. He began to conventionalise his colours. When the pediment or gable of a temple was to be filled with sculpture, it might be, to the observer on the ground and at a distance, no disadvantage to have the background of the walls painted in dark red or some other colour, which would throw up the statues into proper relief, in much the same way as well-regulated and well-provided galleries will put curtains of chocolate-coloured or other velvet behind a marble sculpture which pretends to exquisiteness of outline. We should perhaps admit so much, if we lived in the atmosphere of ancient Greece and looked at the Parthenon marbles up above us, and not, as we are accustomed to do, down upon our own level in a museum. In statuary of excellence the distinctness of outline is everything. A shape of dazzling marble against a white wall or in the middle of a room surrounded by white walls, can never be followed by the eye. The outline is simply confounded and the finest portion of the art wasted.

So much for the painting of the pedimental wall. But for the figures ? It might seem that we could have spared the paint upon them. The older Greek artists, even Pheidias and his school, did not seem to think so. They no longer intended by their colours to make the figures realistic. That fact is obvious inasmuch as their colours became purely conventional. Hair was coloured dark red, sometimes even dark blue; and that is not the colour of hair. A shield might be coloured in dark blue; and that was not the colour of a shield. But it is clear that the artists, not venturing yet to renounce colour, and finding that, viewed from a given distance, the colouring managed to bring out certain lines and details otherwise lost, employed colour simply for that purpose, and as sparingly as they dared.

When wood was abandoned for marble the first blow was dealt to colouring. When the colours became sparing and conventional, merely affecting the hair or the borders of a garment, the second blow was delivered. And when, instead of robed gods seated aloof in shrines, or of scenes of battle depicted aloft on pediments, human beings without drapery were carved for erection close to the eye in wrestling-grounds or other public places, then colouring naturally drew to an end.

Art is evolved, like anything else, and Greek artists learned by experience.

One practice, however, the Greek artists adhered to. The best marble is very dazzling. Therefore every statue in that material was toned down by an application of white wax and oil brushed on, and then made to sink in by heat, after which the surface was rubbed over with a cloth. This does not obscure the texture of the marble, while it does prevent the dazzling and distracting of the eye. In a matter of that kind we may well believe that the Greek sculptor knew his business.

CHAPTER XVII

MODERNNESS OF THE ATHENIAN

CHAPTER XVII

MODERNNESS OF THE ATHENIAN

It should by this time have been brought sufficiently home that the Athenian of the classical time was peculiarly " modern." There are certain respects in which he is far nearer to us, not only than the Roman, but than our own ancestors of a few centuries ago. Despite all the differences of detail in his form of government and administration, his political situation at this period bore no small resemblance to that to which we are coming. So far as parties existed, they correspond very much to our " Labour Party " and its opponents. In respect of law and order it will be remembered that the person of the citizen was most stringently protected. No citizen thought of walking about with a weapon for his own defence. Socially there was an absence of formality and ceremony, which also increases in the present day. In respect of wit and humour Aristophanes and his fellow comedians would be almost as much at home in the twentieth century as in their own. There are scenes and situations which — except that they are in Greek and deal with things Athenian — might have been written by Mr. Gilbert. The irony of Plato is very much that of Matthew Arnold, and the scientific spirit of Aristotle is practically that of Darwin or of Herbert Spencer. The system of two years' training for military service is virtually the modern continental system. The athletic training and enthusiasm of the gymnasia and the

311

public games is being nowadays only too much reproduced. The very appearance of the men was modern.

We must not minimise the differences which have been made apparent. But we may regret a common practice of those who have dealt with antiquity in translations or stories. The practice is no doubt dying out, but it has in the past done much damage to a correct understanding. It is the habit of employing ancient instead of modern terms, quaint old-fashioned expressions instead of current ones, when rendering Greek writers into English, or when speaking of Greek life. The result has been to cast round the ancient Athenian an entirely false atmosphere, to distort his picture, and to put him at a social and intellectual distance which is untrue.

During these chapters we have avoided all the Greek terms and all archaic phraseology, translating, as far as possible by practical modern equivalents. One might have spoken thus : " Pasicles the son of Xanthippus carefully cast his *himation* about him and strode through the *pastas* and *aule* towards the door, followed by his attendant Sosias. ' By Poseidon,' quoth Pasicles, ' it behoves us to hasten ; for it is the time of full market, and haply Lysimachus will have completed his business at the table of Pasias before we can arrive. Hearken, Sosias ; take this *mina* of silver, run with all speed, and deliver it to Lysimachus.' " That is to make Pasicles not only a remote, but rather a stilted person, by a mere fallacy of language. Suppose we express it thus : " Pasicles carefully adjusted his mantle, and strode through the alcove and the courtyard towards the door. Sosias followed. ' Dear me, ' said Pasicles, ' we must make haste : it must be ten o'clock, and I am afraid Lysimachus will have done with his business at Pasias' bank before we can get there. Here, Sosias ; take four pounds, run as hard as you can, and give it to Lysimachus.' "

The sense is exactly the same, but Pasicles and Sosias are brought infinitely nearer to us as human beings. And the important fact is that this effect is true, while the other is false.

The conspicuous mental virtues of the Athenian were intellectual, artistic, and social; a clear intellect, a just perception in art, great social aptitude. His ideal of a man was the man well-educated in mind and body, well-mannered, sensible, tactful; quick to understand a thought or the requirements of a situation; spirited, but temperate. Morally, the cardinal virtues were justice, temperance, wisdom, and courage. A *kalos kagathos* was a fine fellow, a " fine type of man " in all these ways and respects. And many such men there doubtless were. Just and honourable gentlemen were not rare in Athens. Nevertheless one cannot but recognise certain shortcomings. It was not so much that the practice fell short of the theory. That occurs everywhere, and is as common under Christianity as under paganism. It was rather that the moral code did not go far enough. It was the law and good form that controlled action, not some deeper and worthier sentiment of right and wrong. Conscience was not highly developed. There was nothing altruistic about Athenian morality, no doctrine of loving your neighbour as yourself. The Athenian had no religion of charity. For example, in his passionate love of beauty and charm and enjoyment he seems rather to have detested and despised disease and misery than to have pitied it. Limbs ought to be sound and whole and straight ; men ought not to be ill-fed and squalid ; and the average Athenian seems to have resented the obtrusion upon his sight of any violations of these rules. A fine upstanding well-bred man of the world, a quick thinker, with a fair mind, a dislike of excess, and an excellent taste in art and literature — that is a clubbable person whom we are always glad to meet; but there is still something lacking. For thinking and doing he is admirably equipped, but in feeling and its self-sacrifices he may be greatly to seek.

In the intellectual and artistic virtues it is probable that the world has not advanced an inch since Athenian times. Perhaps social intercourse is but little more reasonable or more pleasant. But in the moral attitude of men towards their fellows and themselves there has theoretically been a conspicuous advance. We may believe, too, that the theory may in no slight measure have advanced the practice.

The Athenians would never have aroused and sustained the interest and even enthusiasm with which students regard them, if they had not been a most exceptional people.

They have been compared to various more modern peoples, but only with partial truth. They had, it is true, the artistic creativeness and intellectual enthusiasm of the lively Italian communities of Renaissance times; on the other hand, they had more respect for law, and the illegal and personal violence of poison and the stiletto was comparatively rare among them. They had, it is true, the humour and social readiness, the fluency of speech, the enthusiasm for fine things, which belong to the Celtic Irishman; on the other hand, they had more of cool, coherent, and profound reasoning and sustained creativeness. They had, it is true, the French social tact and love of clear outline and organisation; on the other hand, they had none of the deliberate morbidness in morals which is apt to creep into Parisian literature and life. They had, it is true, the English fondness for athletics and bodily training, but that is the only respect in which we dare compare them with the English. They also bore a very remarkable resemblance in many better respects to the Japanese. What do we get ? A people of admirable physique, of social charm, great artists, clear thinkers, but wanting in certain elements of self-sacrifice, sympathy, and truthfulness, — defects which were partly in the blood, and partly the outcome of a religion which was a peculiar blend of pagan ceremony and a rationalising intellect, but which was nothing more.

INDEX

INDEX

Y